Adobe® Creative Suite 2

CLASSROOM
IN A BOOK®

W9-AMP-385

www.adobepress.com

Adobe

Adobe Press books are published by Peachpit Press, Berkeley, CA. To report errors, please send a note to errata@peachpit.com.

Printed in the U. S. A.

ISBN# 0-321-34982-2

9 8 7 6 5 4 3

Contents

Getting Started

1 Asset Creation and General Setup

2   Designing a CD Cover

3   Creating Distinctive Packaging

4 Publishing a Newsletter

5 Building a Web Site

6 Adding Animation

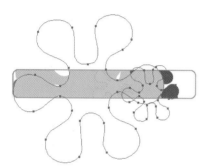

7 Moving from Print to Web

8   Presenting with Style

9   Submitting Work for Review

10   Understanding VC

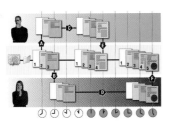

Getting Started

Adobe® Creative Suite 2 is a unified design environment that delivers the next level of integration in creative software. New features and tighter integration among suite components simplify creative and production tasks, enabling you to work more efficiently than ever before. Adobe Version Cue® CS2 includes enhancements in file versioning and review management, while other new features like Adobe Bridge, Adobe Stock Photos, color consistency, and unified Adobe PDF file creation offer greater productivity and collaboration.

The premium version of the Suite combines full new versions of Adobe Photoshop® CS2, Illustrator® CS2, InDesign® CS2, GoLive® CS2, and Acrobat® 7.0 Professional software with new Version Cue® CS2, Adobe Bridge, and Adobe Stock Photos.

The standard version of the Suite combines full new versions of Adobe Photoshop® CS2, Illustrator® CS2, and InDesign® CS2 with new Version Cue® CS2, Adobe Bridge, and Adobe Stock Photos.

About Classroom in a Book

Adobe Creative Suite 2 Classroom in a Book® is part of the official training series for Adobe graphics and publishing software, developed with the help of experts at Adobe Systems. This edition is intended to supplement, not replace, the individual Classroom in a Books for the five products included in the Premium Suite: Adobe Photoshop CS2 Classroom in a Book, Adobe InDesign CS2 Classroom in a Book, Adobe Illustrator CS2 Classroom in a Book, Adobe GoLive CS2 Classroom in a Book, and Acrobat 7.0 Professional Classroom in a Book. We recommend that you also visit www.studio.adobe.com for tips and tutorials on all of the Adobe Creative Suite 2 products and information on other training resources.

This book isn't a complete user's guide to the Creative Suite applications. It takes you step by step through a number of projects, from traditional print work to designing features for the Web. The lessons are designed to let you learn at your own pace. If you're new to Creative Suite, you'll learn the fundamental concepts and features you'll need to get up and running in the programs. If you are an experienced user, you'll learn how to take advantage of Creative Suite's integration capabilities to easily share work between applications. If you want more in-depth instruction on any of the products included in the Suite, you can purchase the corresponding Classroom in a Book or other Adobe Press books.

Although each lesson provides step-by-step instructions for creating a specific project, there is room for exploration and experimentation. You can follow the book from start to finish, or do only the lessons that match your interests and needs. Each lesson concludes with a review section summarizing what you've covered.

Prerequisites

Before beginning to use *Adobe Creative Suite 2 Classroom in a Book*, you should have a working knowledge of your computer and its operating system. Make sure that you know how to use the mouse and standard menus and commands, and how to open, save, and close files. If you need to review these techniques, see your Microsoft® Windows or Apple® Mac® OS X documentation.

Installing Adobe Creative Suite 2

Before you begin using *Adobe Creative Suite 2 Classroom in a Book*, make sure that your system is set up correctly and that you've installed the required hardware and software. You must purchase the Adobe Creative Suite 2 software separately. For system requirements and complete instructions on installing the software, see the *InstallReadMe* file on the installer CD.

Make sure that your serial number is accessible before installing the software; you can find the serial number on the registration card or CD sleeve.

Lesson files . . . and so much more

The *Adobe Creative Suite 2 Classroom in a Book* CD includes the lesson files that you'll need to complete the exercises in this book, as well as other content to help you learn more about the Adobe Creative Suite 2 applications and use them with greater efficiency and ease. The diagram below represents the contents of the CD, which should help you locate the files you need.

What's on the CD *

Here is an overview of the contents of the Classroom in a Book CD

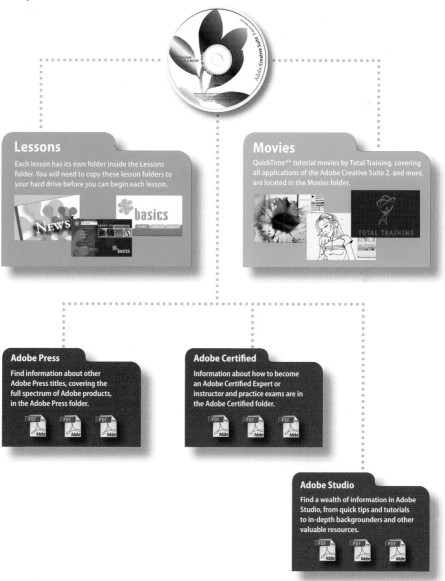

Lessons

Each lesson has its own folder inside the Lessons folder. You will need to copy these lesson folders to your hard drive before you can begin each lesson.

Movies

QuickTime** tutorial movies by Total Training, covering all applications of the Adobe Creative Suite 2, and more, are located in the Movies folder.

Adobe Press

Find information about other Adobe Press titles, covering the full spectrum of Adobe products, in the Adobe Press folder.

Adobe Certified

Information about how to become an Adobe Certified Expert or instructor and practice exams are in the Adobe Certified folder.

Adobe Studio

Find a wealth of information in Adobe Studio, from quick tips and tutorials to in-depth backgrounders and other valuable resources.

*** The latest version of Apple QuickTime can be downloaded from www.apple.com/support/downloads/quicktime652.html.*

Starting the applications of Adobe Creative Suite 2

You start the applications of Creative Suite just as you would most software applications.

For example, to start Adobe Photoshop CS2 in Windows:

1 Choose Start > All Programs > Adobe Photoshop CS2.

2 In the Welcome Screen, click Close.

To start Adobe Photoshop CS2 in Mac OS:

1 Open the Applications/Adobe Photoshop CS2 folder, and double-click the Adobe Photoshop CS2 icon.

2 In the Welcome Screen, click Close.

Copying the Classroom in a Book Files

The *Adobe Creative Suite 2 Classroom in a Book* CD includes folders containing all the electronic files for the lessons in the book. Each lesson has its own folder; you must copy the folders to your hard disk to complete the lessons. To save room on your disk, you can copy only the folder necessary for each lesson as you need it, and remove it when you're done.

To copy the Classroom in a Book lesson files, do the following:

1 Insert the *Adobe Creative Suite 2 Classroom in a Book* CD into your CD-ROM drive.

2 Browse the contents and locate the Lessons folder.

3 Do one of the following:

• To copy all the lesson files, drag the Lessons folder from the CD onto your hard disk.

• To copy only individual lesson files, first create a new folder on your hard disk and name it Lessons. Then, drag the lesson folder or folders that you want to copy from the CD into the Lessons folder on your hard disk.

If you're copying the files in Windows 2000, you may need to unlock the lesson files before you can use them. If you use Windows 2000 and encounter locked files, proceed to Step 4.

This final step is not necessary for Windows XP or Mac OS users.

4 (Windows 2000 only) To unlock the files you copied:

• Right-click the folder that contains the locked files, such as Lessons, and choose Properties from the contextual menu.

• In the Attributes area of the File Properties dialog box, deselect (uncheck) the Read-only check box, and then click Apply.

• In the Confirm Attributes Changes dialog box, select the option "Apply changes to this folder, subfolders, and files."

• Click OK to close the Confirm Attributes Changes dialog box, and click OK again to close the File Properties dialog box.

Note: As you complete each lesson, you will overwrite the start files. If you want to restore the original files, recopy the corresponding Lesson folder from the Adobe Creative Suite CS2 Classroom in a Book CD to the Lessons folder on your hard drive.

Additional resources

Adobe Creative Suite 2 Classroom in a Book is not meant to replace documentation that comes with the program or to be a comprehensive reference for every product in Creative Suite 2. For comprehensive information about program features, refer to any of these resources:

• Adobe Help Center, which is the complete version of the User Guides built into the Adobe Creative Suite 2 applications. You can access Adobe Help Center from the Help menu in the Creative Suite applications.

• Printed User Guides for all the Creative Suite 2 products—Photoshop, Illustrator, InDesign, GoLive, and Acrobat—are available for purchase at www.adobe.com.

• Adobe Studio (www.studio.adobe.com) offers a wealth of information, including tips and tutorials on all the Creative Suite 2 products and links to other offerings from Adobe training partners Adobe Press, Total Training, and Element K.

• The Creative Suite 2 Video Workshop by Total Training, included in your product box. Captured on video, Total Training's instructors lead you step-by-step through key new features and workflows of the Suite.

• Adobe Press offers a wide range of how-to books on all the Creative Suite products. Whether you're a beginner or a seasoned pro, you'll find a book that's right for you.

Adobe Certification

The Adobe Training and Certification programs are designed to help Adobe customers and trainers improve and promote their product-proficiency skills. There are three levels of certification:

• Adobe Certified Expert (ACE)

• Adobe Certified Instructor (ACI)

• Adobe Authorized Training Center (AATC)

The Adobe Certified Expert program is a way for expert users to upgrade their credentials. You can use Adobe certification as a catalyst for getting a raise, finding a job, or promoting your expertise. An exam is required for certification.

If you are an ACE-level instructor, the Adobe Certified Instructor program takes your skills to the next level and gives you access to a wide range of Adobe resources.

Adobe Authorized Training Centers offer instructor-led courses and training on Adobe products, employing only Adobe Certified Instructors. A director of AATCs is available at http://partners.adobe.com.

For information on the Adobe Certified programs, visit www.adobe.com/support/certification/main.html.

The Adobe Creative Suite 2

The Creative Suite 2 combines all of Adobe's flagship design programs into one complete design solution. The Creative Suite 2 Standard includes Photoshop CS2 with ImageReady CS2, Illustrator CS2, and InDesign CS2. The Creative Suite Premium adds GoLive CS2, and Acrobat 7.0 Professional. Both editions also include Adobe Version Cue, an innovative file-management feature, and Adobe Bridge, which serves as the central hub connecting all the applications of the suite.

These are powerful, versatile design tools that have become industry standards: Adobe Photoshop for editing images, Adobe Illustrator for designing graphics and logos, Adobe InDesign for page layout, Adobe GoLive for producing Web pages, and of course, Adobe Acrobat for generating the PDF files that everyone flings around the office to review.

The interaction between these applications has been further integrated and streamlined, adding time- and work-saving enhancements. The applications now share more common commands, tools and palettes, so it's easier to switch back and forth between them. You won't have to pause to remember if you're in Photoshop or Illustrator before you click that mouse.

Additionally, it is now much easier to share your files between applications—often the native file format of one application can be read directly into the next application. No more special exporting and converting when going from Illustrator to GoLive, or from Photoshop to InDesign, which is very helpful, especially if you are going through several review cycles. And to easily share you work with others, you can create Adobe PDF files directly from within the Creative Suite applications.

One of the worst headaches in design work has always been keeping track of all the different versions of your files. This becomes even more important if you work on a project as a team. Adobe Version Cue keeps track for you of who is currently editing which file, revisions can be annotated so everybody in the team can quickly see what changes have been made.

As you use the Creative Suite, you'll discover how each application has been enhanced with new capabilities and features. You will also find the many new templates invaluable for getting started on projects quickly and easily.

The Adobe Creative Suite was developed to make it even easier to work in a world where we hop from one application to another. It combines wonderful design tools into a complete solution for print and web publishing. Using this book as a guide, you'll find it's easier than ever to move files between environments, switch between applications, create design work and output to any medium.

The Adobe Creative Suite 2 applications

Image editing with Adobe Photoshop CS2

Photoshop is the image-editing standard in the field. That's another way of saying it's the application of choice for turning so-so pictures into great ones, using its wide range of tools for airbrushing, line drawing, and adjusting every imaginable parameter of an image. The application is used for a lot more than just editing, though. Designers use Photoshop's sophisticated set of tools to experiment and explore freely, creating all kinds of effects. An integrated Web production application, ImageReady CS2, is included, so you can produce high-quality images for the Web, as well as print and just about any other medium.

Drawing and illustrating with Adobe Illustrator CS2

Illustrator was developed for line art, but designers use it for just about everything. It's wonderfully convenient for creating quick page layouts as well as logos and graphics—just about any single-page document that's not too type-heavy.

Whether you're outputting to print, the Web, or emerging media such as PDA devices, Illustrator is the indispensable tool in your kit.

Page layout with Adobe InDesign CS2

For artwork there's Illustrator. But for brochures, books, anything that uses lots of text, InDesign is where it all comes together. Once your elements are completed in other programs, you can quickly design, layout and print your pages with InDesign. It's surprisingly easy, given the application's power and versatility, because you're using the same intuitive user interface you've come to know in Photoshop and Illustrator.

Not only is InDesign CS2 tightly integrated with the other applications in the Creative Suite, it also has no problems importing styled text documents from Word, converting Excel spreadsheets directly into tables, or importing your previously created page layouts from PageMaker or Quark. Not to mention the range of supported output file formats, like XML, tagged PDF, SVG. And would you mind getting all this with multiple undo and redo?

Web design with Adobe GoLive CS2

Since so much material produced for print also goes out on the Web, it makes great sense to have a Web design program that's integrated with your other publishing tools. With GoLive you can create, manage and deploy powerful Web sites without starting from scratch. Just import the assets you need from Photoshop, Acrobat, and Illustrator. If you use those programs, you'll find Web development in GoLive CS2, with the familiar Adobe user interface, easy and intuitive. GoLive is also well-integrated with InDesign, making true cross-media publishing a reality.

You design your pages using visual layout tools or in source code, as you prefer, going back and forth whenever you want, and previewing your work with the built-in browser. GoLive CS2 gives you design diagrams, tables, and CSS templates to speed up page creation, as well as built-in information architecture tools for designing site maps and other diagrams.

Client review and print output with
Adobe Acrobat 7.0 Professional and Adobe Reader

Adobe Reader is everywhere, and that's what makes PDF such a vital technology. Whenever you want others to see on their screens exactly what you see on yours, a PDF file is the solution. All over the world it's the standard for distributing and reviewing material created from many different sources. Send out a PDF and you can be sure that anyone can view the file, regardless of platform or application.

In the design field, Acrobat 7.0 Professional makes the reviewing process work smoothly. Designers and non-designers will find it easy to start, participate in, and track document reviews, thanks to an easy-to-use How-To window. With the Review Tracker you can keep track of everyone you sent a document to, and what their feedback was.

Everyone can dress up their comments with custom stamps, dynamic date-time stamps, and other drawing tools.

File sharing and versioning with Adobe Version Cue CS2

The bigger the project, and the more people in the review chain, the more likely you'll find that a lot of different versions of your file are floating around. That can get scary, which is why you'll want to check out Adobe Version Cue. It's designed to easily keep track of the many file versions your project may spawn.

Adobe Version Cue keeps the most up-to-date file at your fingertips at all times. But just as easily you can go back to earlier versions of the file if needed. You can scan visually through thumbnails for the file you need, no matter which Adobe Creative Suite application you're in. You can also quickly do a search for keywords, comments, file name, author, date, and more.

You can rest assured that everyone is working on the correct versions of files, and that files won't be accidentally overwritten, sparing you massive amounts of work, energy and frustration.

Organizing assets with Adobe Bridge

Adobe Bridge software is the new navigational control center built for Adobe Creative Suite 2 software and its components. (Adobe Bridge is also available separately in Adobe Photoshop CS2, Illustrator CS2, InDesign CS2, and GoLive CS2 software.) Based on the File Browser introduced in Photoshop 7.0, Adobe Bridge goes a step further by providing centralized access to your suite project files, applications, and settings. With file organization and sharing, plus Adobe Stock Photos, at your fingertips all the time, Adobe Bridge is where you keep your ideas moving.

What's New

Adobe Creative Suite 2 is a unified design environment that delivers the next level of integration in creative software. New features and tighter integration among suite components simplify creative and production tasks, enabling you to work more efficiently than ever before. Adobe Version Cue CS2 includes enhancements in file versioning and review management, while other new features like Adobe Bridge, Adobe

Stock Photos, color consistency, and unified Adobe PDF file creation offer greater productivity and collaboration.

Adobe Photoshop CS2

Revolutionary Vanishing Point

Achieve amazing results in a fraction of the time with the groundbreaking Vanishing Point, which lets you clone, brush, and paste elements that automatically match the perspective of any image area.

Multiple layer control

Select and move, group, transform, and warp objects more intuitively by clicking and dragging directly on the canvas. Easily align objects with Smart Guides.

Smart Objects

Perform nondestructive scaling, rotating, and warping of raster and vector graphics with Smart Objects. Even preserve the editability of high-resolution vector data from Adobe Illustrator software.

Multi-image digital camera raw file processing

Accelerate your raw file workflow with simultaneous processing of multiple images while you continue working. Import images into your choice of formats, including Digital Negative (DNG); enjoy automatic adjustments to exposure, shadows, and brightness and contrast; and much more.

Image Warp

Easily create packaging mock-ups or other dimensional effects by wrapping an image around any shape or stretching, curling, and bending an image using Image Warp.

Adobe Illustrator CS2

Live Trace

Quickly and accurately convert photos, scans, or other bitmap images to editable and scalable vector paths with the Live Trace feature.

Live Paint

Apply color to any region or edge and use overlapping paths to create new shapes with the Live Paint tool, which intuitively colors artwork and automatically detects and corrects gaps.

Control palette

Discover new features and find existing features faster in the context-sensitive Control palette. Accessing selection-based tools from a single location eliminates the need for multiple palettes.

Custom workspaces

Work more efficiently and optimize your screen area using custom workspaces that display only the palettes you need for a specific task. Save, share, or access any workspace at any time or use workspace templates.

Photoshop layer comp support

Control the visibility of layer comps in linked, embedded, or opened Photoshop files from within Illustrator.

Adobe InDesign CS2

Object styles

Apply and globally update object-level formatting more efficiently using object styles. Save a wide range of graphic, text, and frame-level attributes as object styles to create more consistent designs and speed up production tasks.

Adobe Photoshop and Adobe PDF layer support

Selectively display layers and layer comps in Photoshop files, and layers in Adobe PDF files, to experiment with different design options or use multiple variations of a file in your layout—all while linking to a single file.

InDesign snippets

Easily export InDesign objects as snippets, which can be shared with colleagues or reused in other documents. When you place or drag a snippet into a layout, InDesign re-creates the original objects, their formatting, and their relative positioning on the page.

Adobe InCopy CS2 assignments

Assign only the elements of a document that an editor using Adobe InCopy® CS2 software needs to work on while you're designing the rest — whether that's specific frames on a page, frames on one or more spreads, or all the frames in a document.

Save backwards to InDesign CS

Export your InDesign CS2 document to the InDesign Interchange (INX) format and open it in InDesign CS for sharing with people still working in the previous version.

Adobe GoLive CS2

Enhanced live rendering

Preview changes to Web and mobile content in a real-time, integrated engine built on the Opera® browser that supports Small-Screen Rendering (SSR).

Simple visual tools to build and edit CSS-based pages

Build Web pages that conform to open standards using innovative new visual CSS workflows based on the CSS Editor and CSS prebuilt block objects.

Visual CSS authoring for mobile devices

Easily author and validate standards-compliant CSS content for mobile devices using simple visual tools.

Visual SVG-t inspection and authoring for mobile

View SVG-t content in split-view interfaces, enabling art tree, source, and XML outline views and access to an animation scrubbing timeline for rapid development.

Total site management

Track and manage everything in your site, from assets to links, uploading content using Secure FTP and WebDAV via SSH or SSL. Easily synchronize local and remote files.

Adobe Acrobat 7.0 Professional

Inclusive electronic reviews

Use Acrobat 7.0 Professional to enable anyone with free Adobe Reader® 7.0 software to add comments to Adobe PDF files during design reviews.

Improved preflighting of Adobe PDF files

Check for problems in Adobe PDF files using the improved preflighting tool—which now supports droplets for automation—and share preflight reports as comments.

Powerful print production tools

Correct common problems in Adobe PDF files—such as converting colors, previewing separations, remapping spot colors, flattening transparency, and fixing hairline rules—without having to re-create the file.

Ink coverage, rich black detection, and overprint warnings

Minimize prepress errors with new warnings for total ink coverage, rich black detection, and overprints.

Support for the latest standards

Create Adobe PDF files that are compliant with the PDF/X-1a:2003 and PDF/X-3:2003 print production standards, used for prepress document exchanges, and that include JDF product definitions with details about the jobs you're submitting for print production.

Adobe Version Cue CS2

Productivity made simple

Find files fast, track versions across applications, link files together, and share them in creative collaboration without fear of overwriting someone else's work.

Shared project information

Actively track the status of project files and enable this information to be easily shared across workgroups.

Simplified sharing for small workgroups

Easily share files with others within the Version Cue Workspace, and keep your files safe without fear of them being overwritten. View the status of each file to know who is working on what file.

Automatic file naming

Say good-bye to awkward filenames such as brochure_final_final3.indd. Instead, you can name a file to suit your preferences and let Version Cue handle the version tracking without the need for a naming convention.

File version notification

Receive helpful reminders while updating versions or placing photos and illustrations in layouts.

Adobe Bridge

Organized assets

Quickly organize, browse, locate, and preview the assets you need every day—Photoshop images, Illustrator graphics, InDesign layouts, Adobe PDF files, GoLive Web pages, and a variety of standard graphics files—with visual previews and scalable thumbnails as you work.

Project and file sharing

Work collaboratively and access multiple versions as well as alternate renditions of your files through Version Cue CS2 in Adobe Bridge. Actively track the status of project files and enable this information to be easily shared across workgroups.

Accessibility anywhere

Jump to Adobe Bridge from within Photoshop CS2, Illustrator CS2, InDesign CS2, or GoLive CS2, work in it as a standalone application, or have it float onscreen as a palette.

Powerful file searching

Search for files on a hard drive or across a network using extensive metadata information, including attributes such as all files that use a certain PANTONE® color or set of fonts.

Convenient access to stock photos

Browse and search royalty-free images from multiple stock photo agencies using Adobe Stock Photos in one convenient, familiar location. Purchase images from several agencies in a single shopping cart, and manage your imagery without ever leaving Adobe Creative Suite 2.

* basics

Richard Fake (Design God)

* basics
creative solutions

Basics Street 88 | 54800 Basetown | T: 256 53 03 | info@basics.cs2 | www.basics.cs2

The basic elements of a corporate identity, with logo design and color coding, will be developed in this lesson. The assets created here will also form the building blocks for the remaining lessons in the book.

1 | Asset Creation and General Setup

Lesson overview

In this lesson, you'll learn how to do the following:

- Select a color profile.
- Define custom sets of color swatches.
- Create a simple logo in Illustrator.
- Set up a document with a custom page size in InDesign.
- Access the Adobe Help Center.

This lesson will take a little over an hour to complete.

Creating Favorites folders in Bridge

Adobe Creative Suite 2 software ships with Bridge, a new component that serves as the central hub connecting all the applications of the suite. Bridge enables you to browse and preview files on your hard disk, flag files, search for files in various ways, perform batch processes, and much more. Bridge is also the control center for features affecting all other applications in the suite, like the creation of Favorites folders and the selection of color profiles.

As a first step in this lesson, you will use Bridge to copy files from the *Adobe Creative Suite 2 Classroom in a Book* CD to your hard disk.

1   Start Adobe Bridge.

By default, a list of Favorites is displayed on the left side of the Adobe Bridge window.

2   Select My Computer (Windows) or Computer (Mac OS) in the Favorites list.

The content of the selected folder will appear in the large pane on the right. By double-clicking a folder in that pane, you can navigate down one level in the folder hierarchy. Double-clicking a file will open it in the default application, while double-clicking an application icon will launch that application. But, Bridge has more to offer than just the behavior intuitively expected from a file browser.

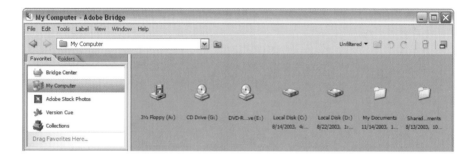

3   Navigate down through the folder hierarchy until you see the contents of the folder in which your documents are usually stored. On Windows, that might be the folder My Computer\Local Disk (C:)\Documents and Settings\username\My Documents and on Macintosh, the folder Computer:harddiskname:Users:username:Documents.

4   Choose File > New Folder, and name the new folder **CS2CIB Lessons**.

5   Click the newly created folder icon, and drag it to the bottom of the Favorites list (or Right-click / Control-click the folder icon, and choose Add to Favorites from the pop-up menu, or select the folder icon and choose File > Add to Favorites).

You've now created a shortcut to the lessons folder that is readily available not only in Bridge, but in all Creative Suite applications.

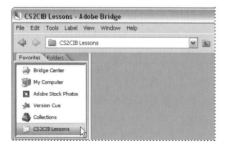

Working with Favorites folders in Bridge

1   Insert the *Adobe Creative Suite 2 Classroom in a Book* CD in the disk drive, click the Folders tab next to the Favorites tab, and select the CD icon in the Folders list.

2   Open the Lessons folder and select the Lesson01 folder in the right pane.

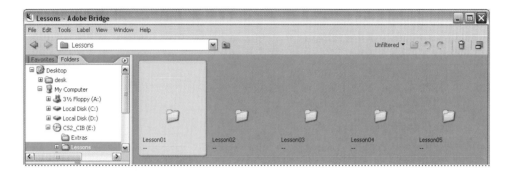

3 Select the Favorites tab, and drag the Lesson01 folder, still visible in the right pane, onto the CS2CIB Lessons folder in the Favorites list.

The folder from the CD will be copied to the hard disk.

4 Click the CS2CIB Lessons folder icon in the Favorites list to see its contents, including the Lesson01 folder.

5 Open the Lesson01 folder, then open the Final folder and select the basics_businesscard.indd file. Choose File > Open With > Adobe InDesign CS2 (default).

InDesign CS2 will launch and open this document, which shows how the business card will look after you work on it in this lesson.

6 Close the businesscard.indd file in InDesign, without saving any accidental changes.

Selecting a color profile in Bridge

Before starting to create any artwork, you should select a color profile to be used by all your Creative Suite applications. This will ensure color consistency throughout the project.

1 If the InDesign CS2 application is still open, choose File > Browse to return to Bridge.

2 In Bridge, choose Edit > Creative Suite Color Settings to bring up the Suite Color Settings dialog box.

The dialog box will show a list of predefined color settings for different workflow scenarios and environments.

3   Select the Show Expanded List of Color Settings Files check box to see additional predefined color settings, in particular, color settings for the European or Japanese markets.

4   For this tutorial, select the North America General Purpose 2 color profile, and click Apply to close the dialog box.

Color Workflow

Accurate and consistent reproduction of color has always been difficult to achieve. The translation of the two most often used color specification models (RGB and CMYK) between devices such as monitor, scanner, or printer often leads to a different color appearance. Adobe Creative Suite 2 offers new color management technologies, enabling more accurate color reproduction. You can read more about this subject in the Color Workflows for Adobe Creative Suite 2 guide provided on the *Adobe Creative Suite 2 Classroom in a Book* CD (Adobe Studio/White Papers/Color Workflows.pdf).

Exploring the color profile settings in Illustrator CS2

You can explore the details of the selected color profile in the individual Creative Suite 2 applications in the same way as shown here for Illustrator CS2:

1   Start Illustrator CS2. If greeted by the welcome screen, click Close.

2   Choose Edit > Color Settings.

In the Color Settings dialog box, the North America General Purpose 2 color profile is selected, and the specific settings of this profile are visible in the lower part of the dialog box.

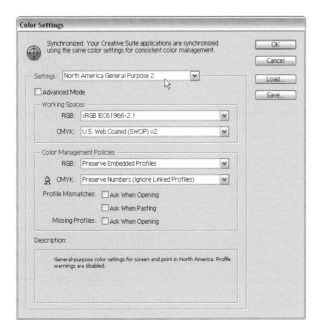

If you hold the pointer over the pop-up menus, you will see additional information about the selected setting, in the Description area at the bottom of the dialog box.

3   Click Cancel to close the dialog box without making any changes to the color settings.

Defining a set of CMYK color swatches

In the course of this book, you will create the artwork for a fictitious graphic design company called Basics. A specific set of colors has been determined to help establish a brand identity for this company.

To facilitate choosing the correct color settings for artwork created in Creative Suite 2 applications, you should define a set of color swatches to be shared by the applications.

1   In Illustrator CS2, choose File > New to bring up the New Document dialog box.

2   Make sure that the CMYK Color Mode is selected, accept the default settings for the Artboard Setup, name the document **basics logo**, and click OK.

3   If the Swatches palette is not already visible, open it by choosing Window > Swatches.

The Swatches palette contains the 46 Default_CMYK swatches, plus [None] and [Registration], which are always the first two swatches in the Illustrator Swatches palette.

4   Click the White swatch (the third swatch from the left after [None] and [Registration] in the top row) to select it, and then Shift-click the global Deep Sea Blue swatch (the last swatch in the last row), to select the entire range of the default CMYK swatches.

5   Choose Delete Swatch from the Swatches palette menu, and click Yes in the dialog box to confirm your intent to delete these swatches.

Don't worry about deleting the default CMYK swatches. They can always be reloaded from the Swatch Library that ships with Illustrator.

Note: The Delete Swatch menu item will not be available if the [None] or [Registration] swatches are part of the selection. Neither of these two swatches can be deleted from the Illustrator Swatches palette.

Adding swatches to your Swatches palette

In the following procedures, you will learn five different ways to add a color swatch to the Swatches palette.

1   In the toolbox, set the Fill and Stroke buttons to their default, and make sure that the Fill button is active (on top of the Stroke button).

2   Click the New Swatch button at the bottom of the Swatches palette. A new swatch (in the current Fill color) will be added to the list in the Swatches palette.

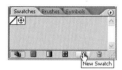

3   Double-click the newly created swatch in the Swatches palette to bring up the Swatch Options dialog box. Name the swatch **Basics Blue**, select Process Color as Color Type, CMYK as Color Mode and enter **83**%, **0**%, **21**%, and **0**% as the CMYK values. Select the Global check box. When you update a global swatch color, all objects using that swatch color are updated accordingly (which is really what we want to have happen, should we ever change the color scheme for the Basics company). Click OK when done.

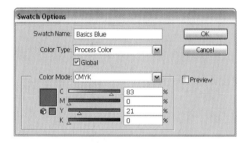

You have created the first custom color swatch. If you hold the pointer over the new swatch, the name Basics Blue will be displayed underneath. The lower right corner of the swatch is white, indicating that the Global option is turned on.

4   To create the second color swatch, choose New Swatch from the Swatches palette menu. The New Swatch dialog box will appear. Call the new swatch **Basics Green** and enter **29**%, **0**%, **100**%, **0**% as CMYK values. Leave the Process Color and Global settings selected. Click OK.

5   To create the third color swatch, double-click the Fill icon button in the toolbox to bring up the Color Picker dialog box. Select **0**%, **53**%, **100**%, and **0**% as CMYK values, and click OK. Now, click the orange Fill icon in the toolbox and drag it over to the Swatches palette. Release the mouse button when the pointer is to the right of the Basics

Green swatch. Double-click the new swatch to bring up the Swatch Options dialog box. Rename it to **Basics Orange**, leave the Process Color setting unchanged, and select the Global check box. Click OK.

6   For the fourth color swatch, select the Basics Orange swatch in the Swatches palette and choose Duplicate Swatch from the palette menu. Double-click the new swatch, and in the Swatch Options dialog box, rename it to **Basics Yellow**, and select CMYK values of **0**%, **16**%, **100**%, and **0**%. Click OK.

7   For the last color swatch, go to the Color palette, choose CMYK from the Color palette menu, and then, if the CMYK sliders are not already showing, choose Show Options from the palette menu to display the CMYK sliders in the Color palette. Change the CMYK settings to **24**%, **56**%, **0**%, **0**%, and then choose Create New Swatch from the palette menu. In the New Swatch dialog box, which looks very much like the Swatch Options dialog box, name the swatch **Basics Purple** and turn Global option on. Then, click OK.

You have created a set of five custom color swatches. The last step is to save this set in the Swatch Exchange file format so that the other Creative Suite 2 applications can import and use it as well.

Saving color swatches for exchange

1   Choose Save Swatches for Exchange from the Swatches palette menu. In the Save Palette as Swatch Library dialog box, click Use Adobe Dialog in the lower left corner. (If the button in the lower left corner reads Use OS Dialog, leave things as they are.)

A view of the files and folders on your computer is displayed, very similar to the one you saw earlier in Bridge. In particular, the CS2CIB Lessons Favorites folder is shown in the list on the left-hand side of the dialog box.

2   Click the CS2CIB Lessons folder icon in the list on the left-hand side of the dialog box to select it. Then, select the Lesson01 folder icon on the right-hand side, and click Open.

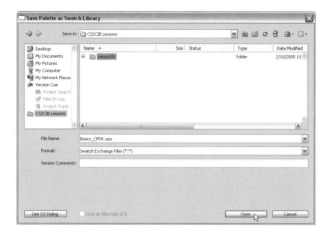

3 Name the file **Basics_CMYK.ase**, make sure the Swatch Exchange File format is selected, and then click Save. Read the Alert about swatches containing gradients, patterns, or tints not currently being exchangeable, and click OK; this is of no importance at the moment since you are only working with regular color swatches.

Tracing artwork

The next step is to work on the logo. Many books have been written about the importance of strategic thinking in approaching branding and logo creation. In this lesson, however, we will tackle only the very last part of this design process: creating the digital artwork of a logo from an existing scanned version of a shape. For this we will use Live Trace, a new feature of Adobe Illustrator CS2, that enables you to convert scanned line-art or bitmap images to vector graphics. More information about this feature can be found in the Creating Vector Content Using Live Trace guide provided on the *Adobe Creative Suite 2 Classroom in a Book* CD (Adobe Studio/White Papers/ Live Trace.pdf).

Instead of creating a perfectly symmetrical and regular shape with one of the Illustrator drawing tools, the starting point for the logo will be an image drawn by hand, and then scanned into Photoshop. The slightly rough and unpolished look will give the logo a more personal touch.

1 With the basics logo file open in Illustrator, choose File > Place. In the Place dialog box, navigate to the Lesson01 folder in the CS2CIB Lessons folder, select the Photoshop file hexa.psd, and click Place.

The scanned image of a flower-like shape will appear on the page. In the following steps, this shape will be called the flower symbol.

2   With the placed image still selected, choose Object > Live Trace > Make and Expand.

The Live Trace command will create two paths, one around the bounding box of the placed Photoshop file, and one around the flower symbol in the middle. Since you're only interested in the inner path, the outer path can be deleted.

3   Use the Direct Selection tool, and select just one point of the outer path by dragging over the top left corner of the image.

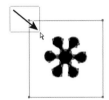

4   Press the Delete key twice, and the outer path will be gone.

As an artifact from the tracing process, the remaining path is still considered part of a group, and is surrounded by a Compound Path. This can easily be cleaned up, and things simplified in the Layers palette.

5   If the Layers palette is not already visible, open it by choosing Window > Layers, or pressing the F7 function key.

6   Click the triangle next to the Layer 1 to expand the view. Expand the view of the Group inside this layer as well. The Path is grouped with a Compound Path.

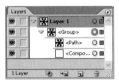

7 Click the word <Path>, and drag it up and out of the group, releasing the mouse when an insertion line appears between Layer 1 and <Group>.

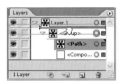

8 Select the <Group> sublayer (now containing only the Compound Path), and click the Delete icon in the lower right hand corner of the Layers palette to delete the selection. Only the path of the flower symbol in Layer 1 will remain.

Applying colors

1 Select the flower symbol on the page with the regular Selection tool.

The Fill and Stroke buttons in the toolbox indicate that the path is filled with black, and not stroked.

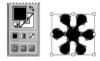

2 With Fill activated in the toolbox, click once on the Basics Blue color swatch in the Swatches palette to create the first building block for the company's logo artwork.

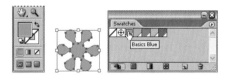

3 With the Selection tool, click the blue flower symbol and keep holding down the mouse button, and then press the Shift and Alt / Shift and Options keys while dragging the selection to the right to make a copy of the symbol right next to the original.

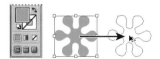

4   Release the pointer, and with the copy of the flower symbol still selected, click the Basics Green swatch in the Swatches palette.

5   With the now green copy of the flower symbol still selected, choose Object > Transform > Transform Again (or simply use the keyboard shortcut Ctrl-D / Command-D) to make another copy to the right of the second flower symbol. Fill the new flower symbol with Basics Orange color, make another copy, fill it with Basics Yellow, and make a final copy in Basics Purple. Click with the Selection tool outside of the artboard, or choose Select > Deselect to deselect all objects.

6   Choose Save As to save your work under the name **basics logo.ai** in Adobe Illustrator file format, in the Lesson01 folder in the CS2CIB Lessons folder. After clicking the Save As button in the Save As dialog box, the Illustrator Options dialog box will come up.

7   Accept all the default settings in the Illustrator Options dialog box. Note the warning messages in the lower part of the dialog box. You will learn more about the raster effect resolution in the following sections. For now, ignore the warning about embedded fonts. Click OK to save the file to disk.

Using a wordmark as part of the logo

Typography and the creation of wordmarks (logos designed only with letters and no images) are other matters well worth spending time on. The best designs derive from a careful typographic exploration, examining the attributes of each letterform and its relationship to others. To get just an idea of the vast variety and classifications of available typefaces, look at http://www.adobe.com/type.

The wordmark for the Basics company has been created in Illustrator, using the font Verve Std Bold in 57 points with a tracking value of +50 applied. For your convenience, the wordmark text has been converted to outlines, and provided in Illustrator file format in the Lesson01 folder.

Note: Do not convert Text to Outlines if this can be avoided. Fonts contain additional information, called hinting, which improves the appearance of text when displayed on a monitor, or printed. The hinting information is lost when Text is converted to Outlines.

1   Choose File > Open, navigate to the Lesson01 folder, inside the CS2CIB Lessons folder, select the file basics_wordmark.ai, and click Open.

2   Choose Select > All (Ctrl-A / Command-A), Edit > Copy (Ctrl-C / Command-C)

3   Choose Edit > Copy (Ctrl-C / Command-C)

4   Choose File > Close (Ctrl-W / Command-W)

5   Choose Edit > Paste (Ctrl-V / Command-V) to place the wordmark artwork in the basics logo.ai document. By default the wordmark will be positioned somewhere in the middle of the page. Move the five colored flower symbols to the top of the page.

6   Select the wordmark and fill it with Basics Blue color.

7   Choose Select > Deselect (Shift-Ctrl-A / Shift-Command-A).

basics

Assembling the logo

1   Select the flower symbol in Basics Green. Hold down the Alt / Option key, and then drag a copy of the flower symbol slightly to the left and above the basics wordmark. *(See illustration on next page.)*

2   With the flower symbol still selected, choose Object > Transform > Rotate, enter **-15** as value for the Angle, and click OK.

3   Click the Basics wordmark to select it. In the Control palette, click the Constrain Width and Height Proportions button, and then enter a width of **190 pt** to slightly enlarge the wordmark. Constrain Width and Height Proportions assures that the height of the wordmark gets scaled proportionally with the width, and the type does not get distorted.

4   Select the Basics Green flower symbol at the left, and choose Filter > Stylize > Drop Shadow.

Note: There are two Stylize entries under the Filter menu, one in the group of Illustrator Filters, and one in the group of Photoshop Filters. Select the Drop Shadow filter from the Stylize submenu in the group of Illustrator Filters.

5   In the Drop Shadow dialog box, select Multiply as Mode, **75%** Opacity, X Offset of **-7 pt**, Y Offset of **5 pt**, and a Blur value of **2.5 pt**.

6   Still in the Drop Shadow dialog box, click the black Color square to bring up the Color Picker dialog box. Click Color Swatches, select the Basics Blue color, and click OK.

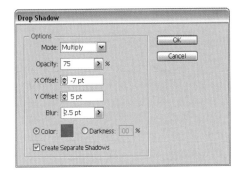

7 Click OK again to close the Drop Shadow dialog box.

8 Choose Select > Deselect, and then save the work.

Transparency

Using transparency features to create see-through effects can help you add interest to your designs. The integration and support of transparency between the applications of Adobe Creative Suite 2 has been further streamlined.

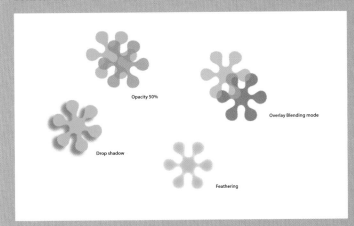

In the "Getting Started with Transparency" guide provided on the *Adobe Creative Suite 2 Classroom in a Book* CD (Adobe Studio/White Papers/Transparency 1.pdf), you will find additional information on working with transparency, and guidelines on choosing (or customizing) flattener presets.

Preparing the artwork for reuse

Now you will define a Crop Area around the logo artwork. When you later place the file in InDesign, you will have the option to place only the artwork within the Crop Area. The Crop Area can also be used to indicate the clearspace, meaning the area that should be left empty around the logo when it is placed in other documents.

1   Select the Rectangle tool, and set Fill and Stroke to None.

2   Draw a rectangle around the logo artwork, leaving some space on either side. Think of this space as the clearspace for the logo design.

3   With the rectangle still selected, choose Object > Crop Area > Make.

Later in this lesson, you will place this logo artwork in its native Illustrator file format into an InDesign document. Using this format has the advantage that the transparency effects remain live, and flattening can be held off until the InDesign document goes to print, or needs to be exported in a flattened format. InDesign's transparency flattener settings will govern how live transparency effects are ultimately flattened.

As a rule of thumb, choose the [Low Resolution] preset for proof prints on a black-and-white desktop printer, the [Medium Resolution] preset for desktop proofs or output on color PostScript printers, and the [High Resolution] preset for printing to imagesetters or high-resolution output devices. For high-resolution output, it is generally best to consult with the print service provider as to which flattener settings to use.

If you want to print artwork containing transparency directly from within Illustrator, or need to output the file in a flattened format (PostScript, EPS, PDF version 1.3 or older), you can select the transparency flattener settings in Illustrator as follows.

4   Choose File > Document Setup, and select Transparency from the pop-up menu in the Document Setup dialog box.

5   Depending on your requirements, select one of the flattener presets in the Export and Clipboard Transparency Flattener Settings section (or create a customized preset), and then click OK.

The logo artwork also contains a drop shadow, which belongs to the group of raster effects. Specifying settings appropriate for the intended use in the Document Raster Effects Settings dialog box is important.

6   Choose Effect > Document Raster Effects Settings.

7   Select the CMYK color model, set the resolution to High, and specify a Transparent background, and then click OK.

8   Save the document. The logo artwork is now ready to be imported into InDesign. Keep the Illustrator file open in the background while working in InDesign, so that a background graphic to be used in the InDesign document can later be easily copied and pasted from the still-open Illustrator file.

Setting up a document in InDesign

1   Start Adobe InDesign CS2.

2   If greeted by the welcome screen, click Close (or click New Document, and then skip step 3).

3   Choose File > New > Document.

4   In the New Document dialog box, leave Number of Pages set to **1**, and set the page width to 3.5 inches and the height to 2 inches (simply type **3.5 in** in the Width field and **2 in** in the Height field, InDesign will take care of converting inches to picas, or

whichever unit is selected as the document's default). You can ignore the settings for Facing Pages and Master Text Frame.

5   Select the Landscape Orientation to have the document appear wider than it is tall. (After you entered 2 inches as height in the previous step, InDesign swapped the width and height entries assuming a standard Portrait orientation.)

6   Leave Number set to **1** in the Columns section of the dialog box, and ignore the value entered as Gutter.

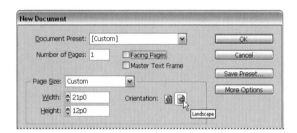

7   In the Margins section of the dialog box, type **0.125 in** (⅛ of an inch) as Top margin, and then click the Make all settings the same icon—the broken chain icon in the center of the Margins section of the dialog box—to quickly apply the same value to all four margins.

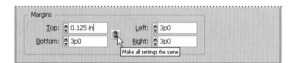

The text on the business card should not be placed outside these margins. Graphical elements like a color bar on the top, however, can be printed right to the edge of the card. For this purpose, you need to set up a bleed area, which is used to align objects that you want to extend all the way to the trimline of your printed document.

Defining a bleed area

1   Click the More Options button to reveal the Bleed and Slug settings area of the dialog box.

2   Type **0.125 in** as Top value for the Bleed, and then click the Make all settings the same icon—at the right-hand end of the Bleed settings—to set the Bottom, Left, and

Right Bleed values to the same measurement. Ignore the Slug settings. (A slug area around the document can be used for additional information related to the document, like instructions to the printer or customized color bar information. Objects in the bleed and slug area of the document are printed, but will be removed when the document is trimmed to its final page size.)

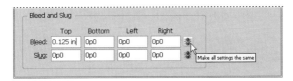

3   Click OK.

InDesign will open a new window with a document the size of a business card.

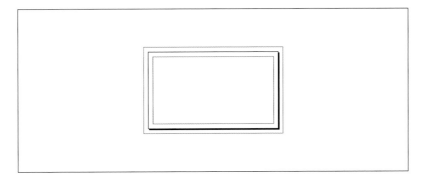

Importing color swatches in InDesign

1   Choose Window > Swatches, or press the F5 function key to open the Swatches palette.

2   From the Swatches palette menu, first choose Select All Unused, and then choose Delete Swatch.

This will clear the Swatches palette of all but the permanent swatches. Next, you will add to the Swatches palette in InDesign the five Basics color swatches you prepared in Illustrator.

3   From the Swatches palette menu, choose Load Swatches.

4   If necessary, switch to the Adobe Dialog version of the Open a File dialog box (if the button on the bottom left reads Use Adobe Dialog, then click it, if it reads Use OS Dialog, then leave things as they are).

5   In the list on the left is the Favorites folder, CS2CIB Lessons. Click it, and then double-click the Lesson01 icon on the right to open it.

6   Select the Basics_CMYK.ase file, and click Open.

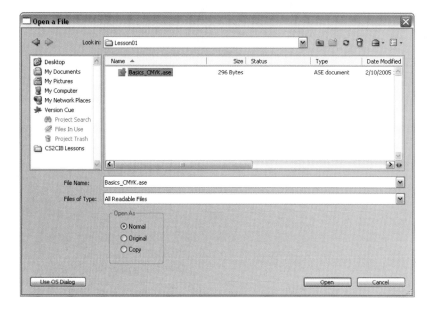

Color swatches for Basics Blue, Basics Green, Basics Orange, Basics Yellow, and Basics Purple will appear in the list of swatches in the Swatches palette.

7   Double-click one of the newly loaded swatches to confirm in the Swatch Options dialog box that the settings have been imported exactly as specified earlier in Illustrator. You will notice the absence of a Global option. All swatches in InDesign behave like global swatches in Illustrator.

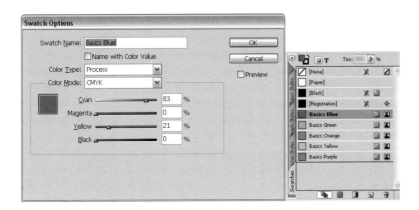

8 Without making any changes to the settings, click Cancel to close the Swatch Options dialog box.

Placing Illustrator artwork

1 To have a better view of the relatively small document, zoom in to about 200%, using either the Zoom tool from the toolbox, or by selecting 200% from the magnification menu at the lower left corner of the document window.

2 Choose File > Place.

3 Note that the Place dialog box opens up in the Adobe Dialog version the way you left the Open a File dialog box in the previous section, with the list of Favorites on the left. Navigate to and open the Lesson01 folder, inside the CS2CIB Lessons folder.

4 Select the Show Import Options check box in the lower part of the Place dialog box. This will bring up an additional dialog box—after clicking Open in the Place dialog box—where (amongst other things) you can specify how to crop the placed artwork.

5 Select the basics logo.ai Illustrator file in the Lesson01 folder, and click Open. *(See illustration on next page.)*

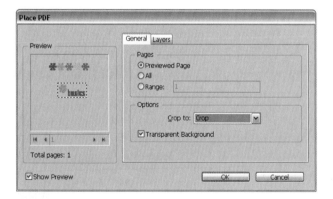

6 In the resulting Place PDF dialog box, select Crop to Crop and turn on Transparent Background under Options in the General panel.

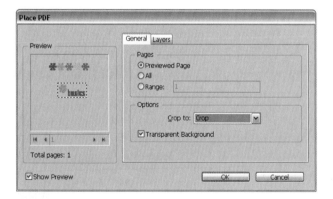

7 Click OK.

8 The pointer takes the shape of a loaded graphics icon. Click anywhere in the top left part of the business card to place the Illustrator artwork.

Scaling Illustrator artwork

The placed artwork will need to be scaled to fit into the space available.

1   With the Selection tool, grab the lower right corner of the bounding box of the placed image, and then hold down the Shift key while dragging the corner point to the left. Holding down the Shift key while dragging the corner point will ensure that the width and height of the bounding box are scaled proportionally.

2   Release the mouse when the bounding box is about 160 points wide. (The current width and height of the bounding box are displayed in the Control palette while dragging the corner point.)

3   With the bounding box still selected, choose Object > Fitting > Fit Content Proportionally (or Object > Fitting > Fit Content to Frame, which would produce the same result here, since the bounding box was scaled proportionally in step 1).

Note: Alternatively, you could have used the Direct Selection tool in Step 1 to select and scale the graphic content of the frame, and then fitted the frame to the content.

4   As guidance for positioning the artwork in the following steps, choose View > Show Rulers. Right-click / Control-click the horizontal ruler, and choose Points from the pop-up menu. Do the same for the vertical ruler.

5   With the Selection tool, click inside the bounding box of the placed and scaled artwork to select it, and then click and drag it into position. The top left corner of the bounding box should be positioned approximately 40 points down and 25 points to the right from the top left corner of the business card.

Note: Alternatively, a selected frame can be positioned in the Control palette by choosing a reference point, and entering x and y coordinates.

6   Choose Edit > Deselect All.

7   Choose File > Save

The Save As dialog box will come up because the file has not yet been saved.

8   In the Save As dialog box (using the Adobe Dialog version), navigate to and open the Lesson01 folder, inside the CS2CIB Lessons folder, choose the InDesign CS2 document file format, name the file **basics_businesscard.indd**, and click Save.

Adding more graphical elements

1   With Fill activated in the toolbox, select Basics Green as foreground color in the Swatches palette.

2   Set Stroke to None in the toolbox.

3   Select the Rectangle tool in the toolbox and click once at the top left corner of the bleed guides.

4 In the Rectangle dialog box enter **270 pt** as Width and **30 pt** as Height. When done correctly, this rectangle should extend to the right edge of the bleed area and overlap the top of the document by 21 points.

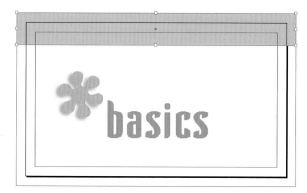

5 Switch to, or start, Illustrator, and open the file basics logo.ai, if it's not still open.

6 With the Selection tool, click the Basics Blue flower symbol in the top right corner of the document, and choose Edit > Copy.

7 Switch back to InDesign.

8 Choose Edit > Deselect All if the rectangle is still selected, and then choose Edit > Paste.

Adjusting the design

A big blue flower symbol appears in the center of the document window. Note that a new color swatch was added to the Swatch palette. The CMYK settings for this new swatch are the same as those for the Basics Blue color swatch, which is as it should be. You can assign the Basics Blue color swatch to the placed image, and then eliminate this redundant new color swatch.

1   With the placed flower symbol still selected, activate the Fill button in the toolbox, and then select Basics Blue from the Swatches palette. If necessary, activate the Stroke button in the toolbox and set the stroke width to None.

2   Choose Edit > Deselect All.

3   In the Swatches palette, select the newly added (and now redundant) blue color swatch, named c83m0y21k0 after its CMYK values, and click the Delete Swatch icon in the lower right corner of the Swatches palette to delete it.

4   Use the Selection tool to select the Basics Blue flower symbol.

5   Using the Control palette, scale the flower symbol proportionally by **250%**, rotate it by **-15** degree, and position its center at X: **180** pt and Y: **80** pt.

6   Open the Transparency palette, and set the Opacity to **25%**.

7   As a last step to use this flower symbol as background image, choose Object > Arrange > Send to Back.

8   Choose Edit > Deselect All, and save the work.

Adding text

1   In the toolbox, select the Type tool.

2   In the Control palette, select the font Myriad Pro (which is installed automatically with InDesign CS2), in Bold, and 10-point size.

3   Make sure that Snap to Guides is turned on (View > Grids & Guides > Snap to Guides), and that the Guides—in particular the document's margins—are visible (View > Grids & Guides > Show Guides).

4   Click the top left corner of the document's margin guide (visible through the green bar at the top of the business card), and drag to the right and down to create a text frame approximately 200 points wide and 20 points high. As an alternative, you can type in those dimensions into the Control palette.

5   With the cursor blinking in the top left corner of the text frame, set the text color to white (named [Paper] in the Swatches palette) and type **Richard Fake** (with a space after the name), change the font to Myriad Pro Regular 6 pt, and type **Design God**.

6   In a similar manner, create a text frame at the lower edge of the business card, stretching from left to right margins, and about 20 points high. Select Myriad Pro Regular 7 pt, and with black selected as the text color, type the contact details **Basics Street 88 | 54800 Basetown | T: 256 53 03 | info@basics.cs2 | www.basics.cs2** into the text frame.

7   Tracking can be adjusted to shrink or expand text that is just a tiny bit too long or too short to fit the text frame width. To adjust the tracking, select the entire line and set the tracking to -**5**. Finally, use the Selection tool and move the text frame so that the text baseline sits just above the lower margin of the business card.

8   Add a third text frame about 100 points wide and 20 points high, underneath the wordmark, and flush with the right margin. Set the text color to Basics Orange, set the font to Myriad Pro Bold 12 pt, and type **creative solutions**.

9   Select Align right in the Paragraph palette (Window > Type & Tables > Paragraph).

10 Use the Selection tool to select this last text frame, and then use the up and down arrow keys to adjust the vertical position of this tag line underneath the wordmark.

11 Save the work when done.

Getting help

Another new application besides Bridge in Creative Suite 2 is Adobe Help Center. This application can be accessed by choosing Help > InDesign Help (or the respective menu command in the other applications of the suite). This central application provides convenient access to product help for GoLive, Illustrator, InDesign, Photoshop, and even for Adobe Help Center itself. And through Adobe Help Center, finding out more about Adobe Expert Support and links to other online resources is only one click away.

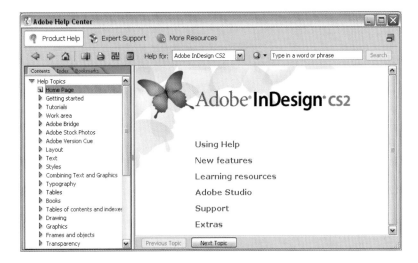

Review

▶ **Review questions**

1 Describe at least three ways to create a color swatch in Illustrator?

2 How can scanned images be converted to vector graphics in Illustrator?

3 How does CS2 help you to achieve consistent colors across applications and platforms?

4 How can you share custom color swatches between Illustrator and InDesign?

5 How can you choose how artwork is cropped when placed in InDesign?

▶ **Review answers**

1 Click on the New Swatch button in the Swatches palette, choose New Swatch from the Swatches palette menu, drag the Fill icon from the toolbox onto the Swatches palette, select a swatch in the Swatch palette and choose Duplicate Swatch from the palette menu, choose Create New Swatch from the Color palette menu, copy an object from another document with it's own color swatch. You can also load swatches from other Illustrator files and swatch libraries.

2 Use Illustrator's new Live Trace feature.

3 Creative Suite 2 ships with a color management system that is turned on by default. Global color profiles control the applications' color management settings. You can choose between several predefined color profiles to account for typical working environments, or you can adjust them for your particular needs. Sharing color swatches in the Adobe Swatch Exchange file format helps to maintain consistent color across the CS2 applications.

4 Choose Save Swatches for Exchange from the Swatches palette menu to save your set of swatches in the Adobe Swatch Exchange file format. Then, import this file by choosing Load Swatches from the Swatches palette menu in InDesign. Swatch files in the Adobe Swatch Exchange file format can be read by CS2 versions of GoLive, Illustrator, InDesign, and Photoshop.

5 In the Place dialog box, select the Show Import Options checkbox. Then, in the following dialog box, choose how the placed artwork gets cropped.

Logo Design

Corporate Identity

Illustration

Photography

Print Material

Web Design

Interactive Design

Animation

ABOUT US

basics

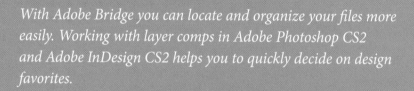

With Adobe Bridge you can locate and organize your files more easily. Working with layer comps in Adobe Photoshop CS2 and Adobe InDesign CS2 helps you to quickly decide on design favorites.

2 | Designing a CD Cover

Lesson overview

In this lesson, you'll learn how to do the following:

- Access Adobe Stock Photos through Bridge.
- Browse and rank images using Bridge.
- Create layer comps in Photoshop.
- Preview layer comps in InDesign.

This lesson will take about an hour to complete.

In Lesson 1, you set up a folder called CS2CIB Lessons on your hard disk. For this lesson, copy the Lesson02 folder from the *Adobe Creative Suite 2 Classroom in a Book* CD into the CS2CIB Lessons folder.

Working with Adobe Stock Photos

Bridge is a sophisticated file browser and a control center for managing global features like the selection of color profiles and the creation of Favorites folders—as seen in Lesson 1. Bridge also provides convenient access to a feature called Adobe Stock Photos, which enables you to search for high-quality, royalty-free stock images from some of the world's leading stock image libraries, and download low-resolution comp images for evaluation purpose. A high-resolution version of the image can be purchased directly from within the Adobe CS2 applications.

Note: Adobe Stock Photos is an online service. To browse and purchase images, you require a working Internet connection. Even if there is no working Internet connection at the moment, it is still possible for you to access Previous Searches, Downloaded Comps, and Purchased Images offline.

1   Start Adobe Bridge.

2   Click Adobe Stock Photos in the Favorites list on the left.

The main screen that will appear on the right (the picture might look different on your computer, as Adobe Stock Photos gets updated regularly), explains how to take advantage of this feature in the design process. You can see a list of stock photo providers, browse images by categories, and search across all libraries by keywords.

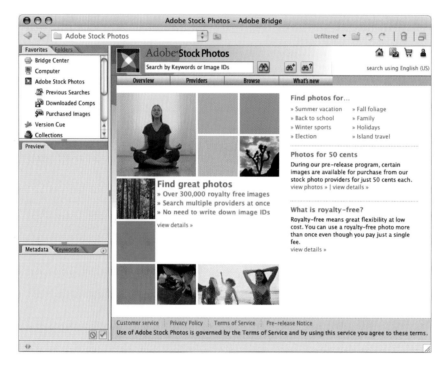

Let's say you need an image of an orange-colored fish for your next project.

3   Type **orange fish** in the search field under the Adobe Stock Photos logo. To start the search, press Enter (Windows) or Return (Mac OS), or click the magnifying glass icon to the right of the search field.

In an instant, the first 50 results of the search will be displayed as thumbnail images. If there are more results available, they can be appended to the list of thumbnails by clicking the More Results button. The number of results to be returned each search can be specified in the Adobe Stock Photos panel of the Bridge Preferences dialog box.

4   Select one of the thumbnail images by clicking it. Your images may vary from those shown in the next few steps.

To see a larger preview of the selected image, drag the divider lines between the panes to enlarge the preview pane on the left.

5   Click the Get Price & Keywords button at the top of the search results pane.

Note: The first time you try to get price and keyword information, you will be prompted to select the billing country so that the prices can be listed in the local currency. Choose the country name from the pop-up menu, and then click Continue.

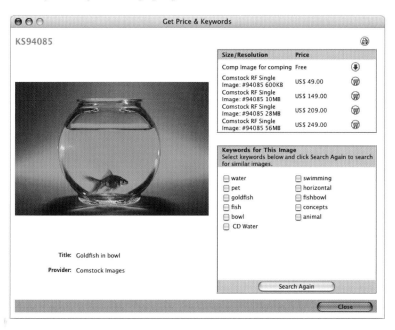

The images are generally available in various sizes, at different price points, the higher the resolution the higher the price. Low-resolution comp images can be downloaded for free. This will enable you to compare different comp images in the document before making a purchase decision.

If desired, you can search for more images using the same, or a subset of, the keywords associated with this image.

6   For now, just close the Get Price & Keywords dialog box by clicking Close.

Next to the Get Price & Keywords button, at the top of the search results pane, there are two more buttons, labeled Download Comp and Add to Cart. These buttons enable you to directly download a comp image, or add the image to your shopping cart. The desired image size can be selected when you review the shopping cart before proceeding to the check out.

7   Click the Download Comp button next to the Get Price & Keywords information button. You may select for this dialog box not to come up in future.

8   Click the View Downloaded Comps button, or Click OK, and then select Downloaded Comps under Adobe Stock Photos in the Favorites list. The selected image will show up in the right pane.

In the Movies/Creative Suite 2 folder on the Adobe Creative Suite 2 Classroom in a Book CD, you will find a movie called Bridge & Stock Photos.mov, further explaining the of use Adobe Stock Photos in Bridge.

Examining metadata

You will now use Bridge to add a copy of this comp image to the project folder.

1   Click once on the downloaded comp image thumbnail in the right pane to select it.

2   Choose Edit > Copy.

3 Click CS2CIB Lessons in the Favorites list.

4 Double-click the Lesson02 folder icon on the right to open it.

5 Choose Edit > Paste.

A copy of the file will appear inside the project folder. Even though it appears to be just a regular JPEG file, Bridge recognizes it as an image comp file, and provides access to additional information associated with the image.

6 Right-click / Control-click the copy of the image comp in the project folder to bring up the context sensitive pop-up menu. Keep the mouse pressed down and examine the menu entries. Note the various choices that would not be available when Right-clicking / Control-clicking a regular JPEG file. In particular, there are now menu items to request additional pricing and keyword information, and to add a high-resolution version of the image to the shopping cart.

7 Choose File Info from the menu to display the metadata panel for this file.

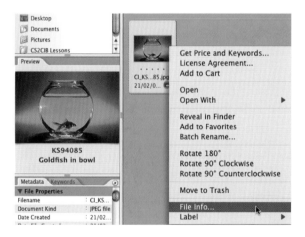

Bridge knows that this JPEG file is a comp image because of additional metadata stored with the file. Even if the file is renamed and moved around on the hard disk, Bridge will remember the original name, the media ID, the image provider, and much more. Bridge enables you to see (and even add to and alter) the information that is stored with the file. In connection with metadata, you may have heard the acronyms XML and XMP. These acronyms refer to the particular data format in which the additional information, the metadata, is stored within the file.

8   For an example of metadata stored with a comp image file, click the Stock Photos entry in the list on the left to see the media ID and the stock photo library provider associated with this file. When purchasing a stock image, the purchase and transaction IDs will be stored here as well.

9   Click Cancel to close the panel without making any changes to the metadata.

In addition to Bridge, the other Creative Suite 2 applications can also parse the metadata stored for comp images. For example, when a comp image is placed in InDesign CS2, an icon on the Links palette identifies it as an Adobe Stock Photos Comp image, and the Links palette menu offers an additional option, Purchase this Image. If you select this option, a high-resolution version of the image will be placed in your shopping cart, ready for order review and check out.

Viewing and ranking images in Bridge

1   In Bridge, open the CD Cover Images folder, inside the Lesson02 folder, inside the CS2CIB Lessons folder.

You will see three Photoshop files that are candidates for use on the cover of the CD Label that you will create in this lesson. Note that you don't just see generic icons of the files, but thumbnail views of the actual content of the files. The size of these thumbnails can be adjusted with the slider at the bottom of the window. At the lower right side of the window are buttons you can use to toggle between Thumbnails view, Filmstrip view, Details view and Versions and alternates view. This feature enables you to choose the best viewing mode for your review needs and preferences.

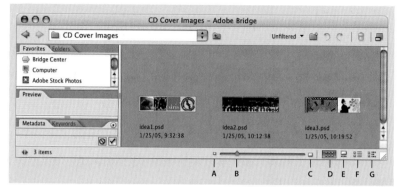

A. Smallest thumbnail size. **B.** *Thumbnail size slider.* **C.** *Largest thumbnail size.* **D.** *Thumbnails view.* **E.** *Filmstrip view.* **F.** *Details view.* **G.** *Versions and alternates view.*

2   Click the Details view button in the lower right corner of the window.

This view confirms that all files have the same size and resolution and are saved in CMYK color mode.

To quickly scan and pre-select a large number of images in a folder (such as the photos downloaded from a digital camera after a studio shooting), the images can be rated using the slideshow mode, in combination with the number keys 1 through 5 on the keyboard. When done, Bridge can display the images sorted by rating.

3   Choose View > Slide Show to switch to the Slide View mode. While in Slide View mode, press the H key to display the slide-show keyboard shortcuts, and press H again to hide them.

4   With the first image visible on screen, press a number key between 1 and 5 to assign a rating. Click the right arrow key to display the next image (or wait for the image to appear after the default delay of 4 seconds), assign a rating, and continue this procedure until reaching the end of the slide show.

With only three pictures in this folder it's probably not so obvious, but this can be a real time-saver if there is a large number of images to go through.

5   Deselect View > Sort > Ascending Order to toggle it off. Then choose View > Sort > By Rating. *(See illustration on next page.)*

If there were more images to choose from, you could select the three highest ranked images to use in the next step.

6   Select the three images by choosing Edit > Select All.

7   Choose File > Open With > Adobe Photoshop CS2 (default).

Photoshop will start up and open the three images.

Creating a multi-layered document in Photoshop

Layer comps is a feature that was introduced in Photoshop CS. New in Creative Suite 2 is the support for layer comps in InDesign CS2.

Layer comps enables you to define design variations for a multi-layered Photoshop file, and then quickly switch between layer comps to review the alternate versions of the design. In each layer comp, the visibility, position and appearance of all layers in the document can be adjusted. If you are familiar with ImageReady's frame animation feature, those layer comps can be thought of as being like individual frames in an animation. Just as flipping through frames is used to animate a design, flipping through layer comps is a quick way to review design alternatives.

In this lesson, you will create a very simple layer comp by turning on and off the visibility of layers for each layer comp. To learn about more creative ways to use layer comps, search for "layer comps" in the Adobe Help Center under Help for Photoshop, or consult the tips and tutorials section in Adobe Studio (http://studio.adobe.com), or Photoshop's *Classroom in a Book*.

Adobe Bridge Modes

While working in the other Creative Suite 2 applications you can keep Adobe Bridge open in Full Mode in the background, ready for you to jump to and use to locate and open files. Or you can switch Bridge to Compact or Ultra-Compact mode by clicking the respective buttons in the upper right corner of the Bridge browser window. Both compact modes display Bridge as a floating palette, visible while you're working in a different application. Compact mode shows thumbnail previews of the selected folder. Ultra-Compact mode displays only the Go back and Go forward buttons and the Recent Folders menu. As soon as you start to navigate to a folder in Ultra-Compact mode, Bridge automatically switches to Compact mode so that you can see thumbnail previews. Both modes provide a button to toggle back to Full mode.

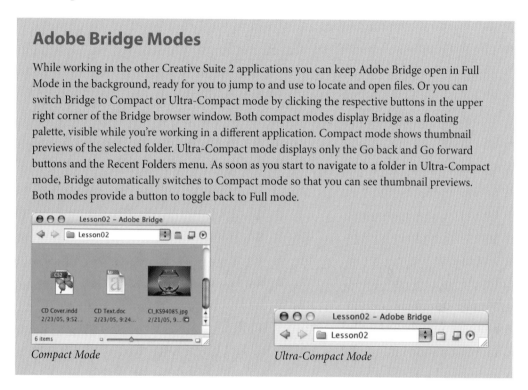

Compact Mode   *Ultra-Compact Mode*

To define layer comps, a multi-layered document is needed. You will now create a new, multi-layered document, with one layer for each of three design alternatives.

1   In Photoshop, choose Window > idea1.psd to bring this document to the foreground.

2   Choose Select > All, and then choose Edit > Copy.

The clipboard now contains the attributes of the current document, which can be used to create a new document with the same resolution, color mode and size.

3   Choose File > New, name the new document **CD Cover Comps**, and select Clipboard from the Preset pop-up menu.

New

Name: CD Cover Comps

Preset: Clipboard

Width: 1104   pixels

Height: 283   pixels

Resolution: 250   pixels/inch

Color Mode: CMYK Color   8 bit

Background Contents: White

Advanced

OK
Cancel
Save Preset...
Delete Preset...

Image Size:
1.19M

4   Make sure that Background Contents is set to White, and click OK.

5   With the new document now in the foreground, choose Edit > Paste.

This will create a new layer containing a copy of the content from the idea1.psd document. Create two more layers for the two other designs as follows:

6   Select the idea2.psd document, choose Select > All, and then Edit > Copy.

7   Select the CD Cover Comps document, and choose Edit > Paste.

8   Repeat steps 6 and 7 for idea3.psd.

You have created a document with one layer for each design alternative. The image in the topmost layer is hiding the other images below.

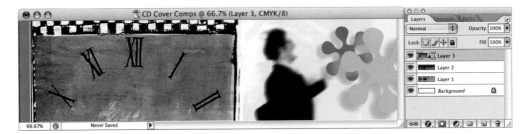

Creating layer comps in Photoshop

Now your work will be to create three layer comps, selecting a different design to be visible in each one.

1   In the Layers palette, click the eye icons at the left of the two top-most layers to hide them.

Only the content of Layer 1 should now be visible in the document.

2 Choose Window > Layer Comps to open the Layer Comps palette.

3 With only the content of the Layer 1 and Background layers visible in the document, click the Create New Layer Comp button at the bottom of the Layer Comps palette.

4 In the New Layer Comp dialog box, make sure the Visibility check box is selected, and then click OK. If you work with more complex documents, it is generally a good idea to give each layer comp a meaningful name and a brief description.

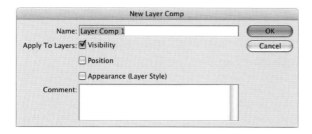

5 In the Layers palette, make Layer 2 visible. Since the image in Layer 2 completely covers the content of the image underneath, there is no need to turn off the visibility for Layer 1 and hide it. However, as a matter of best practice, and to clearly indicate your design intention, turn off the visibility of Layer 1 anyway.

6 With only Layer 2 now visible in the document, click the Create New Layer Comp button at the bottom of the Layer Comps palette.

7 In the Layer Comp dialog box (Window > Layer Comps), make sure that the check box next to Visibility is selected, and then click OK.

8 In the Layers palette, make Layer 3 visible, hide Layer 2, and then create a third Layer Comp as described above.

You can switch quickly between the three-layer comp versions of the document by clicking the Apply Previous Selected Layer Comp, or Apply Next Selected Layer Comp arrow buttons at the bottom of the Layer Comps palette. *(See illustration on next page.)*

In this case, only the visibility of the layers changes, but in general, using layer comps enables you to adjust the visibility, position, and appearance of all layers in the document with a single click. To clean up the work area before moving on, close the Photoshop windows of idea1.psd, idea2.psd, and idea3.psd.

Saving a Photoshop file containing layer comps

You save a file containing layer comps in the same way as saving any other file when the layers should be preserved. Just make sure to leave the check mark selected next to Layers in the Save As dialog box. Photoshop will then automatically store information on how to adapt the layers for each layer comp.

1   Choose File > Save As.

2   If the Save As dialog box is not already set to the Adobe Dialog version, click the Use Adobe Dialog button at the bottom left of the Save As dialog box. If the button reads Use OS Dialog, leave things as they are.

3   Click CS2CIB Lessons in the list of Favorites on the left.

4   Double-click the Lesson02 folder icon on the right to open it.

5   Make sure to select Photoshop from the Format pop-up menu, leave the check boxes selected next to Layers, and ICC Profile (Windows) or Embed Color Profile (Mac OS), and then click Save to save the file under the name **CD Cover Comps.psd**.

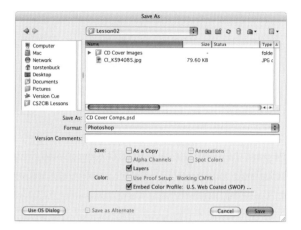

6   If the Photoshop Format options dialog box appears, then leave the Maximize Compatibility selected, and then click OK. This dialog box can be turned off in Preferences under File Handling.

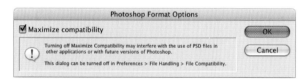

Reviewing layer comps in InDesign

1   Still in Photoshop, choose File > Browse (or click the Go to Bridge button in the Options palette) to switch to Bridge.

2   In Bridge, locate the file CD Cover.indd in the Lesson02 folder, insider the CS2CIB Lessons folder on the hard disk. Click the file icon to select it, and then choose File > Open With > Adobe InDesign CS2 (default).

The InDesign CS2 application will start up and open the file CD Cover.indd. This document, with custom size and slug area, has been prepared to utilize the assets created in Lesson 1. All that is left is to place the Photoshop file on the front of the CD cover, and to import and style some text for the back. Guides are already defined to help you with placing the Photoshop image and text.

3   In InDesign, choose File > Place.

4   Switch to the Adobe Dialog version of the Place dialog box, if necessary.

5   Navigate to the Lesson02 folder, inside the CS2CID Lessons Favorites folder.

6   Select the file CD Cover Comps.psd, which you just saved from within Photoshop.

7   Deselect the check boxes next to both Show Import Options and Replace Selected Items, and then click Open.

8 The pointer takes the shape of a loaded graphic icon. Move the pointer towards the point where the two guides cross just below the text ABOUT US. Click the page to place the image.

The image will fit nicely into the space reserved for it in the cover design. The image of the layer comp that was selected when saved in Photoshop is shown. To see how the other layer comp images would look in its place, do the following:

9 With the newly placed image still selected, choose Object > Object Layer Options.

10 Position the Object Layer Options dialog box on the screen in order to see at the same time both the dialog box and the document window with the cover design.

11 Select the check box next to Preview, and then flip through the different layer comp versions, by selecting them from the Layer Comp pop-up menu.

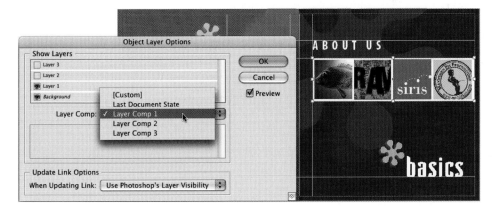

12 Select the layer comp that you think works best for the design, and then click OK.

13 Choose Edit > Deselect All.

Importing text from word processor documents

Not only is InDesign well integrated with the other Creative Suite applications, but it also enables you to import text and graphics in numerous formats, including native Word and Excel files. When importing text from a Word document, you have the choice to ignore or preserve text styles and formatting, or match imported styles with styles defined in InDesign. In this lesson you will simply import unformatted text from a Word document, and leave the formatting to InDesign.

1 Choose View > Grids & Guides > Hide Guides.

2 Choose View > Show Frame Edges.

You can now see a text frame placed on the purple reverse side of the CD cover design.

3 With the Selection tool, click anywhere inside the text frame on the purple background to select it.

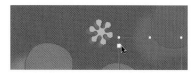

4 With the text frame selected, choose File > Place.

5 Select the file CD Text.doc in the Lesson02 folder, inside the CS2CID Lessons Favorites folder. Don't double-click yet.

6 Select the check box next to Show Import Options.

7 Select the check box next to Replace Selected Items.

8 Click Open.

The Microsoft Word Import Options dialog box will appear because the Show Import Options was selected in step 6.

9 Leave all the check boxes selected in both the Include and Options sections. In the Formatting section, select Remove Styles and Formatting from Text and Tables.

To learn more about preserving style and formatting information from a Word document when importing text into an InDesign document, please refer to the movie called Importing Word files.mov in the Movies/InDesign CS2 folder on your Adobe Creative Suite 2 Classroom in a Book CD.

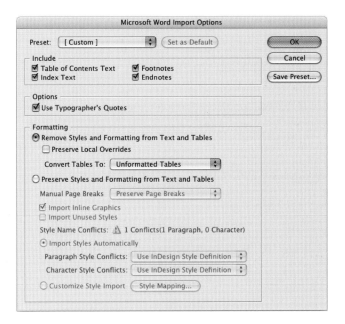

10 Ignore all the other options offered and click OK.

The text will flow directly into the previously selected text frame because the Replace Selected Items in step 7 has been clicked. Be careful when loading text this way into a frame that is not empty. The text will be inserted at the current cursor location, replacing any text that happens to be selected when the Place command is invoked.

Because you selected to disregard the text formatting from the Word document in step 9, the text will be formatted using the text attributes that were defined for the text frame created in InDesign.

11 Choose File> Save, name the file **CD Cover Final.indd** and save it in the Lesson02 folder, inside the CS2CIB Lessons Favorites folder.

Review

▶ **Review questions**

1   What are the advantages of working with Adobe Stock Photos?

2   What are the differences between the Compact and Ultra-Compact modes of Adobe Bridge?

3   What is a quick way to rate a large number of images in Adobe Bridge?

4   How can layers be hidden in Photoshop?

5   What is the advantage of using layer comps?

▶ **Review answers**

1   Adobe Stock Photos are easily accessible via Bridge. You can search for high-quality, royalty-free stock images from leading stock image libraries and download low-resolution comp images for evaluation purposes. High-resolution versions of the images can be purchased directly from within Adobe CS2 applications.

2   The Ultra-Compact mode displays only the Go Back and Go Forward buttons and the Recent Folders menu, while Compact mode shows thumbnail previews of the content of the selected folder.

3   To quickly rate a large number of images in a folder, you can use the slideshow mode in combination with the number keys 1 through 5 on your keyboard.

4   In the Layers palette, click on the eye icon on the left side to make it invisible, and to hide the layer. The content of a layer is also invisible if it is under another layer that does not have any transparent areas.

5   Layer comps facilitate the process of showing different design solutions. While linking your artwork to a single file, you can select and display layers and layer comps in Photoshop files and Adobe PDF files.

Cellared and bottled by
Chalet Wines, Inc., Napa Valley, Calif
Don't call us, we call you. Your business is very importar

This Merlot wine is soft and warm on the palate. Rich ar
but only moderately tannic. Its dark, rich and strong arc
clude scents of plums and black cherry.
Recommended as accompaniment to lamb and simply p
beef dishes.

Government Warning
Government warning, gove
warning, government warni
ernment warning, governm

How do people decide what to buy?

*Often it's the packaging. The design of a box,
label, or bag can make or break a product in the
marketplace.*

*The combination of Adobe Illustrator and Adobe
Photoshop provides you with powerful tools to
create great labels.*

3 Creating Distinctive Packaging

Lesson overview

In this lesson, you'll learn how to do the following:

- Resize, crop and change the resolution of photos in Photoshop.
- Use Photoshop's color modes for special effects.
- Define crop marks, layers, guides and clipping masks in Illustrator.
- Place photos and add text and graphics in Illustrator.
- Use Illustrator's Brushes and Symbols.
- Create a 3D comprehensive (dummy) of a bottle and map artwork.

This lesson will take about an hour to complete.

In Lesson 1, you set up a folder called CS2CIB Lessons on your hard disk. For this lesson, copy the Lesson03 folder from the *Adobe Creative Suite 2 Classroom in a Book* CD into the CS2CIB Lessons folder.

In this lesson, your project is to design a label for a wine bottle. You will use Photoshop to prepare a background image, and then do the layout in Illustrator, placing the background image and adding text and other graphics. Finally, you will preview the label design on a 3D comprehensive of a bottle.

There are a number of items that have to be included on this label. The front of the label must display the brand name; this will be "Chalet," and the product name, "Merlot." Grape leaves are the theme for the graphics on the front of the label. On the back of the label will be general facts about the winery, any legally required text, and additional information about the wine.

You will start this project by creating the image used as the background pattern on the front of the label.

Resampling Images

Resampling is the process of changing the number of pixels in an image. *Upsampling* increases the number of pixels while *downsampling* reduces it.

The lower-resolution image can't be as detailed as the higher resolution image—with *downsampling* you lose information as you reduce the file size. That's OK in some cases, such as when displaying pictures on screen, where a resolution of 72 ppi (pixels per inch) is normal.

There are various methods the computer can use to calculate the color of each pixel in the resampled image, based on the color of each pixel or group of pixels in the original image.

You can choose between *Nearest Neighbor* (which is a fast but relatively unsophisticated algorithm), *Bilinear* (moderately fast and medium quality), and *Bicubic* (which is slower but yields smoother tonal gradations).

Upsampling (from lower to higher resolution) is not a good idea if you have a low-resolution picture that you want to print at a higher resolution. No matter how smart the resampling algorithm, it can only fake a higher resolution by interpolating pixel information. This process can't create more detail than is present in the original image. For printing purposes, you should always start with an image of high enough resolution. Downsampling is OK (though it can also result in poorer image quality), but where quality is an issue, upsampling should be avoided.

There are circumstances where upsampling comes in handy, of course, such as when playing your DVD movies full-screen on a laptop computer.

Changing dimension and resolution of a photo in Photoshop

The concept for this wine label is to have a picture of grape leaves as a background pattern for the text on the front of the label. A digital photo of grape leaves will serve as a base to add more artistic design modifications. You could search for a picture of leaves in Adobe Stock Photos, or, as an alternative, simply use the one provided on the *Adobe Creative Suite 2 Classroom in a Book* CD.

1   Start Photoshop and open the file leaves.jpg in the Lesson03, folder inside the CS2CIB Lessons folder.

This is a picture taken with an inexpensive digital camera of some ivy. The size is 1600-by-1200 pixels, but some cropping needs to be done before it can be used. For the wine label, the image size needs to be about 6.3-by-2.36 inches. In general, the resolution should be at least 250 to 300 ppi for a photo that needs to be printed. For our purpose (to convert the picture to a background pattern), a resolution of 200 ppi is more than enough. For a 6.3-by-2.36 inch image at 200 ppi, an image area of 1260-by-472 pixels completely covered with leaves is necessary. Don't worry; Photoshop can do the math for you.

2   Choose Image > Image Size to bring up the Image Size dialog box.

3   In the Image Size dialog box, make sure the check box next to Resample Image is deselected, and then set the Resolution to **200** pixels/inch. *(See illustration on next page.)*

This will merely change the number of pixels printed per inch, but not change the image itself.

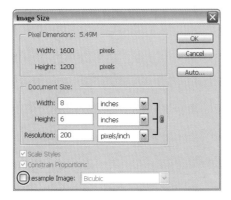

4 Click OK to close the Image Size dialog box.

5 With the Rectangular Marquee tool selected in the toolbox, choose Fixed Size from the Style pop-up menu in the Options palette. Enter **6.3 in** as Width and **2.36 in** as Height.

6 Click somewhere on the left side of the image. A selection marquee rectangle will appear. Click it and drag it around to find an area completely covered by leaves. Then choose Image > Crop.

Turning a photo into an abstract background image

Now you'll change the realistic photo of leaves into a more abstract image. This is meant to be only a backdrop image, not the main focus of the label design. With this in mind, the number of colors will be reduced, and matched to the colors used later on in Illustrator for the other artwork on the label.

1 In the toolbox, click the Default Foreground and Background Colors icon to set the foreground color to black and the background color to white.

Black and white works best to get the desired result from the filter that you will use. Deciding which filter and what colors to use certainly requires some experimenting. Photoshop's Filter Gallery (Filter > Filter Gallery) is a great feature to use to create a desired effect.

2 Make sure that either nothing or the entire image is selected, and then choose Filter > Sketch > Chalk & Charcoal (or choose Filter > Filter Gallery, and then select Chalk & Charcoal from the Sketch group).

3 Set the Charcoal Area value to **12** to enhance the dark areas. Leave the Chalk Area value at **6** and set the Stroke Pressure value to **2** to increase the contrast a little. You can see the effect of the current settings in the big preview pane on the left. Click OK to close the dialog box and to apply the filter to the image.

You can create a nice effect by assigning specific colors for the dark and light areas of the picture. This can be achieved by taking a little detour: temporarily changing the image mode to Duotone, and picking the colors before finally converting the picture into CMYK Color mode.

4 To be able to select Duotone from the Image > Mode dialog box, first change the image to Grayscale by choosing Image > Mode > Grayscale. Click OK if a dialog box pops up asking you to confirm that you want to discard the color information.

5 Now choose Image > Mode > Duotone. In the Duotone Options dialog box, select Duotone from the Type pop-up menu. Click the square color icon for Ink 1 to bring up the Color Picker dialog box. (If the Color Libraries dialog box comes up instead, click the Picker button to switch to the Color Picker dialog box.) Enter CMYK values of C: **31**, M: **45**, Y: **100**, and K: **9**, and then click OK. Type **brown** as the name for Ink 1. In the same way set Ink 2 to C: **0**, M: **33**, Y: **100**, and K: **0**, and name it **orange**. Click OK to close the Duotone Options dialog box. *(See illustration on next page.)*

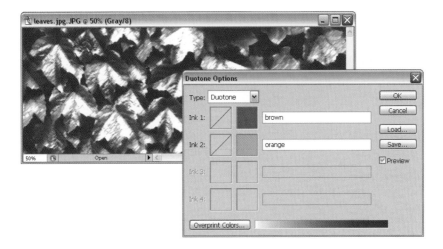

6   Choose Image > Mode > CMYK Color.

7   Choose File > Save As. In the Save As dialog box, navigate to the Lesson03 folder, inside the CS2CIB Lessons folder on your hard disk, select Photoshop as Format, name the file **background.psd** and click Save.

Designing a label in Illustrator

1   Start Illustrator, and choose File > New. In the New Document dialog box, select Letter from the Size pop-up menu, click the Landscape Orientation button, and choose CMYK Color Mode. Name the document **winelabel.ai**, and click OK.

You will now create a black rectangle as background for the wine label, and set up crop marks the same size as the rectangle.

2   Select the Rectangle tool from the toolbox and click once somewhere near the left edge of the page. In the Rectangle dialog box enter **700 pt** as Width and **190 pt** as

Height (if you don't have Points selected as your document's default units, Illustrator will automatically convert the values you enter to these units), then click OK. Using the Selection tool to drag the rectangle, position it in the middle of the page.

3 In the Layers palette, select Layer 1 and choose Duplicate "Layer 1" from the Layers palette menu.

4 Still in the Layers palette, click the Layer 1 target indicator (the small circle to the right of the layer name). This will select the rectangle on Layer 1.

5 Choose Object > Crop Area > Make.

6 In the Layers menu, double-click the Layer 1 name to bring up the Layers Options dialog box. In the Layers Options dialog box, name the layer **crop marks** and click OK.

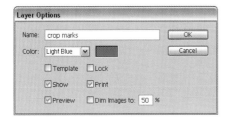

7 Double-click the Layer 1 copy name in the Layers palette and, in the Layers Options dialog box, change the name to **background** and click OK.

8 Choose the Selection tool and select the rectangle in the background layer.

9 With the Fill button activated in the toolbox, click the Black swatch in the Swatches palette. Activate the Stroke button in the toolbox and set it to None.

Now you have created a black rectangle on which you will place the images and text.

10 Choose File > Place. Locate the file background.psd in the Lesson03 folder, inside the CS2CIB Lessons folder. Make sure Link is selected, and then click Place. *(See illustration on next page.)*

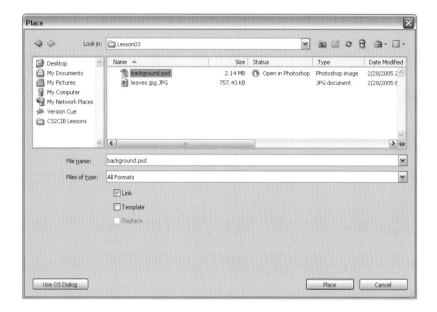

Illustrator will place the image in the center of your document window.

11 Using the Selection tool, position the placed Photoshop image towards the left end of the black rectangle as shown in the illustration below. You can use the arrow keys on the keyboard to make some fine adjustments to arrive at the final position.

12 Choose File > Save As. In the Save As dialog box, select Adobe Illustrator (Windows) or Illustrator document (Mac OS) as Format. Save the document as **winelabel.ai** in the Lesson03 folder, accepting the default settings in both the Save As and Illustrator Options dialog boxes.

Adding guides, graphics, clipping masks

The next step is to concentrate on the two main elements for the front of the label, the brand name, Chalet, and the wine type, Merlot. For a start, you will draw a burgundy-colored circle on which the type will later be placed.

1 Make the rulers visible in the document window by selecting View > Show Rulers, or holding down the Ctrl / Command key while typing R.

2 If it's not still selected, select the placed image with the Selection tool, bringing up two diagonal lines crossing at the center of the image.

3 Create a vertical guide by clicking the vertical ruler and dragging the pointer to the right. Release the pointer when the new vertical guide aligns with the center of the placed image. Now, the front part of the label has been marked with a guide that will help you later on to position other design elements of the label. When done, deselect the placed Photoshop image.

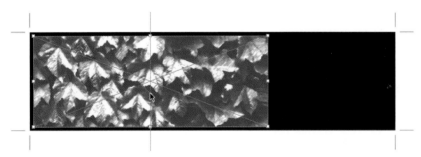

4 In the Layers palette, create a new layer on top of the background layer and call it **graphics**.

5 With the graphics layer selected in the Layers palette, double-click the Fill icon in the toolbox to bring up the Color Picker dialog box. Specify a burgundy color with the CMYK values C: **25**, M: **100**, Y: **90**, K: **25**, and click OK.

6 Activate Stroke in the toolbox and set to None.

7 Select the Ellipse tool in the toolbox.

Note: The Ellipse tool is hidden behind the Rectangle tool in the toolbox. To find it, click the Rectangle tool icon and hold down the pointer, and then select the Ellipse tool from the menu that comes up. Using the keyboard shortcut L can also activate the Ellipse tool.

8 Click (don't drag!) anywhere on the page to display the Ellipse dialog box. Enter **200 pt** for both the Width and the Height, and then click OK. A burgundy colored circle should appear on the graphics layer in front of the background image.

9 With the Selection tool, drag the circle so that its center aligns vertically with the newly created guideline, and sits horizontally just above the lower edge of the label. You can also use the arrow keys on the keyboard to nudge the circle into final position.

10 Deselect the circle.

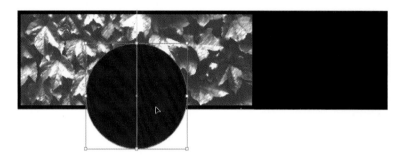

To visually cut off the part of the red circle that extends beyond the label area, define a clipping mask:

11 Using the Rectangle tool, with Fill and Stroke set to None, draw a rectangle covering the top part of the circle and flush with the bottom edge of the label as shown in the illustration below. If necessary, the arrow keys can be used to reposition the rectangle after the pointer has been released.

12 Leaving the rectangle selected, use the Selection tool and Shift-click the circle to select both objects. Choose Object > Clipping Mask > Make. Only the part of the ellipse that lies within the rectangle remains visible.

13 Choose Select > Deselect to deselect all when done.

Adding text

Before starting to add text to the label, consider carefully what sort of typeface will work best. To get a feel for which typeface best suits the brand name, it's good to try several fonts. For Chalet, the font Voluta Script could be used to evoke the feel of a noble, old winery steeped in tradition. Also, its handwritten appearance gives the wine label a more personal feeling. The word "Chalet," typed using Voluta Script Pro Regular in 70 point size, and then converted to outlines, is provided in the file chalet.ai in the Lesson03 folder. If you have your own copy of Voluta Script installed on the system, use that instead of placing the file in step 2 below.

For the product name, Merlot, and the body text, visually balance out the script typeface Voluta with a more formal serif typeface like Minion Pro, which is inspired by classical, old style typefaces of the late Renaissance, a period of elegant, beautiful, and highly readable type designs.

Both the winery name and product name will be set reversed out of the burgundy-colored round shape. Chalet picks up the golden color from the background image, and Merlot will be in plain white to set it apart.

1   In the Layers palette, create a new layer above the graphics layer, and call it **type**.

2   With the type layer selected in the Layers palette, choose File > Place. Navigate to the Lesson03 folder. Select All Formats from the Files of type (Windows) or All Readable Documents from the Enable (Mac OS) pop-up menu. Select the file chalet.ai and click Place. In the Place PDF dialog box, choose Crop from the Crop to pop-up menu and click OK.

3   Using the Selection tool and the arrow keys on the keyboard, position the word Chalet horizontally centered in the top half of the circle. *(See illustration on next page.)*

OpenType

OpenType gives you access to the magic of good typography, through a vast array of features that make your typesetting more refined and professional looking. OpenType is a new font format that combines the benefits of PostScript Type 1 and TrueType fonts. The font files are cross-platform, which means that you can use exactly the same files on a Windows PC and a Macintosh.

All information is contained in a single file. No more screen font files with separate outline or metrics files. Furthermore, one font file can contain all the glyphs that previously had to be stored in separate expert font files—swash, ornaments, or fractions fonts. In fact, a single OpenType font file can contain more than 60,000 glyphs. This not only comes in handy for large character set fonts, such as those for Chinese or Japanese languages, but also for Western fonts that might contain hundreds or even thousands of glyphs to meet high quality typesetting requirements.

(Continued on next page.)

4 Deselect all, and then select the Line Segment tool from the toolbox. Set the Stroke color to C: **0**, M: **25**, Y: **80**, K: **4** (the same color as used for the word Chalet). Set the Stroke Weight to **2.5** point in either the Control or Stroke palette, and then draw a straight line under the word Chalet. Deselect all. *(See illustration on next page.)*

InDesign, Illustrator, and Photoshop are equally well equipped to take advantage of the new features offered by OpenType fonts. Illustrator even offers a dedicated palette for easy access to OpenType features (Window > Type > OpenType).

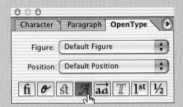

A Glyphs palette in both InDesign and Illustrator lets you find and access every glyph available in the font. Here you might just find the special version of a glyph needed for your task at hand, like the 't' with the high crossbar used in the word Chalet in this lesson,

To learn more about OpenType and good typography, check out http://www.adobe.com/type. This site will provide you with more practical knowledge about type design and type setting, so you can fully appreciate what OpenType technology has to offer.

Holding down the Shift key constrains the drawing of lines to horizontals, verticals, and 45° angles.

5 Select the Type tool in the toolbox. In the Character palette (Window > Type > Character), select the font Minion Pro Bold, 18 pt. Set the tracking to 150.

Titles or headings in all capital letters are best set with extra letter spacing (tracking).

6 Click underneath the word Chalet (there is a blinking cursor on the page), set the Fill color to White, and type in capitals the word **MERLOT**.

7 Use the Selection tool and the arrow keys to optically center the word MERLOT, and the word Chalet.

8 Select the word Chalet, the line underneath, and the word MERLOT, and use the arrow keys to center the group optically within the circle. In this case, hiding the centered guideline might actually help to better optically balance these elements. When done, deselect all.

Note: The Align palette (Window > Align) aligns objects relative to their bounding boxes, but this alignment is not always optically centered, especially if you work with asymmetrical shapes.

Using Illustrator's brush and symbol libraries

As a final touch, you will add some images of leaves around the burgundy-colored circle, which will tie in well with the background image. For this, you can take advantage of Illustrator's brush and symbols libraries, which include a vast selection of ready-to-use artwork, including some nicely drawn leaves.

1 Choose Window > Symbol Libraries > Nature. Click the Maple Leaf Large symbol in the Nature palette, and then drag and drop it onto the page. A copy of the leaf artwork will appear on the page. Close the Nature palette to save space on the screen.

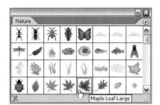

You could manually add several of these leaf symbols to the design or, as shown in the following steps, use the symbol as a brush, and have Illustrator reiterate the leaf design along a path.

2 With the leaf artwork still selected, choose New Brush from the Brushes palette menu. In the New Brush dialog box, select New Scatter Brush, click OK, and then in the Scatter Brush Options dialog box that follows, click OK again, accepting the default settings.

The leaf artwork has now been added to the Brushes palette.

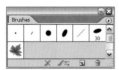

3 Delete the one instance of the leaf artwork still selected on the page.

4 Choose the Ellipse tool from the toolbox, and set Fill and Stroke to None. Draw an ellipse, wider than it is tall, around the red circle. *(See illustration on next page.)*

Note: While dragging, hold down the Space bar to reposition the ellipse.

5 With the ellipse still selected, click the leaf in the Brushes palette.

Several leaf images will appear along the path of the ellipse. You can control how the images are placed along the path in various ways, by changing options in the Scatter Brush Options dialog box.

6 Double-click the leaf image in the Brushes palette to open the Scatter Brush Options dialog box. Select the check box next to Preview, and position the dialog box so that the dialog box and wine label can be seen at the same time.

7 Select Random from the pop-up menu for Size. Now enter the values for the minimum and maximum scale factor. Enter **170%** and **180%**, respectively. For Spacing, choose Random, **100%** and **160%**, for Scatter, choose Random, **-60%** and **-45%**, and for Rotation, choose Random, **30°** and **65°**. Select Rotation relative to Path in the pop-up menu. Leave the other options unchanged, and click OK. Since the options for the brush have been changed after being used on the ellipse path, the Brush Change Alert will come up. Click Apply to Strokes.

You have now designed a frame of leaves on top of the type layer, which enables you to better see the effects while working in the Scatter Brush Options dialog box. The ellipse should be moved to where it belongs, behind both the text and the burgundy-colored circle.

8   With the frame of leaves still selected, choose Edit > Cut. Select the graphics layer in the Layers palette, and choose Edit > Paste in Back. When clicking the triangles next to the layers' names in the Layers palette, you can see the stacking order of the elements on the page. Alternatively, you could have dragged the Path with the leaves from the top of the type layer to the bottom of the graphics layer in the Layers palette.

The next step is to create another clipping mask, to have these leaves be visible only in front of the background image.

9   Deselect all. Use the Rectangle tool with Fill and Stroke set to None, to draw a rectangle the size of the Photoshop image placed in the background.

10   In the Layers palette, drag this new path just above the path with the leaves in the graphics layer. Click its Target Indicator, and then Shift-click the target indicator of the path with the leaves. With both paths targeted, choose Object > Clipping Mask > Make. The final appearance of the work can always been checked by selecting View > Preview. *(See illustration on next page.)*

11 Leave the now-clipped frame of leaves selected, and choose Effects > Stylize > Drop Shadow (from Illustrator Effects). In the Drop Shadow dialog box, choose Multiply from the Mode pop-up menu, set the Opacity to **80%** and X and Y Offset both to -**10 pt**. Leave Blur at **5 pt** and Color Black, and then click OK. Save your work.

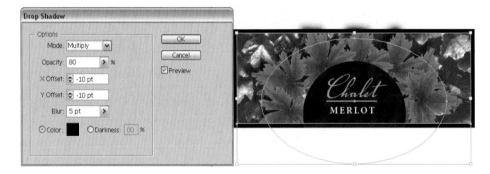

Only a few things remain to be done: designing the layout for the label back, and doing minor refinements to the front. A file called winelabel_refined.ai, with all these final adjustments already done, is provided in the Lesson03 folder.

With packaging design in particular, it is usually best to use a restricted number of carefully chosen fonts and colors. This will help avoid the different elements competing with each other.

This also assists to establish a hierarchy of information. In the case of the wine label, the brand name should be read first, followed by the product name, and then the year. Another advantage is to accommodate the possibility of product line extension: Should Chalet also produce a Sauvignon wine, the color coding could simply be changed by replacing the burgundy circle with another color. This way, Chalet would retain its already-established look and help to build brand recognition.

Creating a 3D comprehensive

To present the packaging label, or to quickly check out different structural designs, Illustrator has a great feature, the three-dimensional (3D) effect. This will enable you to transform two-dimensional artwork into three-dimensional objects. For example, you will now turn the drawing of an outline of a bottle shape into a realistic looking 3D comprehensive. Since 3D Revolve is implemented as an Effect, modifying the outline will result in a different bottle shape.

A simple line drawing of a wine bottle is the starting point to create a 3D comprehensive or mock-up. The Lesson03 folder contains an Illustrator file prepared for this purpose. The color of the line drawing determines the color of the bottle—in this case a bottle green hue.

1 In Illustrator, open the file called bottle-drawing.ai, located inside the Lesson03 folder, inside the CS2CIB Lessons folder.

In the top part of the document there is a line drawing of the outline of half a bottle. At the bottom of the page is an image of the label you have just created.

2 With the Selection tool, select the line drawing in the top part of the page, and then choose Effect > 3D > Revolve.

3 In the 3D Revolve Options dialog box, turn on Preview, and then without changing any settings for now, click OK. *(See illustration on next page.)*

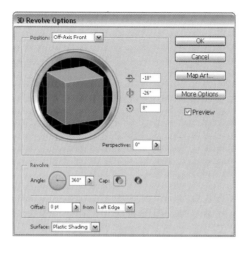

That's it! You've designed a 3D comprehensive of a wine bottle. Of course the bottle would look nicer if the label could be attached to it. This will be the next step.

Mapping artwork

To get a first impression of how the label will look on a bottle, the artwork can be mapped on the 3D model. For a quick reference, a lower resolution version of the original Illustrator artwork is sufficient and helps save processing time.

1 With the Selection tool, click the image of the wine label in the lower part of the document to select it, and then drag it over the Symbols palette (Window > Symbols), and release the pointer.

You have added a new symbol to the Symbols palette.

2 Double-click the new symbol in the Symbols palette to display the Symbols Options dialog box. In the Symbols Options dialog box, rename the new symbol to **winelabel,** and click OK.

3 Click the wine bottle to select it, and then double-click 3D Revolve in the Appearance palette to open the 3D Revolve Options dialog box.

4 In the Symbol Options dialog box, select Preview, and then click Map Art.

5 Select Preview in the Map Art dialog box, and then select surface number 12 of 18 by clicking the arrow icons next to the word Surface.

6 Select the winelabel symbol from the Symbol pop-up menu.

The image of the winelabel will appear in the surface mapping area of the Map Art dialog box, and you can see in the document window a preview of the label mapped to the wine bottle.

7 Click the winelabel image in the Map Art dialog box, and drag it to the left edge and upper half of surface 12. Then, click the center handle on the right side of the label, hold down the shift key, scale the image to be flush right with the surface, and release the pointer.

8 Click OK to close the Map Art dialog box.

9 In the 3D Revolve Options dialog box, use the position tools to rotate the bottle to get a nice view of the front of the label, and then click OK.

Done! Now you have a good idea of how the label will sit on the bottle, and what further refinements might be needed. However, the best way to check is (and will always be!) to print out the label, wrap it around a real glass bottle, hold it in your hands and place it next to other bottles. Nothing's better than the real thing!

Review

▶ **Review questions**

1 When is it a good idea to downsample an image?

2 What are the advantages of using a duotone instead of simply converting an image to grayscale?

3 How can you check out the different character sets and alternate glyphs of an OpenType font?

4 How do you find the different Libraries in Illustrator?

5 How do you map artwork to the surface of a 3D object in Illustrator?

▶ **Review answers**

1 Downsampling, which means to reduce the number of pixels used to define an image, is especially useful when moving from print to Web. For a good quality print, an image with 250 dpi or more is needed, but for viewing on screen a lower resolution of 72 ppi is sufficient and the file size can be reduced by downsampling the image. Important to understand is that downsampling reduces the information (pixels) stored in an image. You cannot recover this lost information once the image has been downsampled.

2 A duotone, a color photograph printed in only two colors, has a greater tonal range than a grayscale image, which is printed in just one color. While a Photoshop image can contain 256 levels of gray, a printing press might reproduce as few as 50 levels of gray per ink. The additional color information of the two inks of the duotone adds more depth to the image, and makes its appearance less coarse. In the example of the wine label the duotone provides a richer background than just a grayscale image, picking up key tones in the center of the image. Duotones in sepia colors often evoke often an impression of past-time photography—and for the wine label this conveys the quality of an old, noble product.

3 The Glyphs palette displays all the characters and character variants included in an OpenType font, given that the font design has been provided with them.

To open the Glyphs palette in InDesign, you choose Type > Glyphs or Window > Type & Tables > Glyphs. In Illustrator, choose Type > Glyphs. Photoshop has access to the OpenType features if you select Window > Character, but it does not offer a Glyphs palette.

4 Illustrator comes with a wide variety of preset brushes, graphic styles, swatches and symbols. To view the different libraries, choose Window, and select Brush Libraries, Graphic Style Libraries, Swatch Libraries or Symbol Libraries.

5 To map artwork to a 3D object, add the image you want to use to the Symbols palette, select the 3D object, and double-click 3D Revolve in the Appearance palette to open the 3D Options dialog box. Click the Map Art button. Select the Surface to map the artwork to, and then choose the image from the Symbol pop-up menu. The image can then be positioned and scaled on the selected Surface in the Map Art dialog.

NewsLetter

Vanishing Points!

NEWS

Odo iure dolore velodigniam iure dolore vel ullan odigniam iure iure dolore vel velismod deliquisi. *(page 2)*

EVENTS

Lendipsumsan ut nit ullamet num volore volobore facip erciliq uissit iure dolore vel pratet non exer secte volore volobore facip erciliq uissit iure. *(page 2)*

PROGRAM

lum volesequipis ex volore volobore facip erciliq uissit iure ero ex eros alis dolummy nim del dignim quisim dio et ilis leniam augait. *(page 3)*

OPINIONS

volore do odolore minit loborperos niam vel et volore volobore facip erciliq uissit iure adit numsan utat prate vullum incidunt. *(page 3)*

CALENDAR

volore volobore erciliq uissit iure adit numsan utat prate facip erciliq uissit iure full page calendar *(page 4)*

Unt aliquisi. Uptat. Guer si et, con ut nosto core magna feuguercil dolor susci et alit incil erciliquis nonsequatet duis nis augiam, cortissequi bla consed duisse feuip exerit at nonsendrero dolenim ipit velis nostio estis autpat pratue dit eugait wisl incillan ulluctat, vullum zzrit ut nos dipisi tat lore veliqui sseut nos dipisi tat lore veliqui sseut nos dipisi tat lore veliqui ssequis non ullamet alissit acipism quis non ullamet vullaore te con ent oloreetum vullaore te con ent veliscinim aut praesti onumsan ea commy nostrud eumsandreet aliquisi.

Onsed ming er sequi tat ilit ullaore tio er at nisisl et ute cor secte dolorer sequat velesto delit praestrud etue dolorem zzriure magna alisi enibh eugue venim dio con ut dolobor in utpat el do erciliquamet nim zzrit iure vendigna aliscin vel utet adit volortisi tat, volore modipsuscip eu facilis nosto dolent nos nosto corper amconsenibh eugueros dolore velis nim inci tio euis et venim verate tem dolor irilla consequat, vent lorem nulla faccum duis at volorem zzrit ex eugue faccum dunt veniscin hendrem nulla faccum nostrud ercidunt lut lorerostrud duisisl eugue magna alisl ullam, conse-eugue magna alisl ullam, consequis ad et la feuguer ad mod dolore diametuerit ute ero odolobo rercill amcore vel inciduisl do ea faccum volum dolenisis nonse-

quam, susto esenit la feu feum ad euisi.

Bore tem quate ea conum velessit adigna alit ver iuscil ipsusci lismodo luptate tat, vulla autpat lobore molendi pisisci er sis dit laore mincidunt vendipis alit, quam quipismod er iniam, commod ex euguero core do eugiam, vulluptat nibh et lobortio odignim essi tat. Ut at laorperit dolorem in esed doluptate eu feu facinibh enibh eum vent wisim iureet niat, quismodit ver am nis nummod tat, sectet, consed ercin henisl ing eratuerilla commy num nonsecte dolum quis dunt lum volore magna facin ullut velendreet prat ea adip er ing eugait alit luptat alit lum zzrit ea feugait nis niamet, quat. Duis ea conse duipissecte cor susto elisi.

Liquis nim vullumsan ullummo dolore ero consed ratio consenim acilla feugait nibh et, quismod doluptat ate dunt praesenis doleniam alit ver ingore tem quate ea conum velessit adigna alit ver iuscil ipsusci lismodo luptate tat, vulla autpat lobore molendi pisisci er sis dit laore minciidunt vendipis alit, quam quipismod et iniam, commod ex euguero core do eugiam, vulluptat nibh et lobortio odignim essi tat. Ut at laorperit dolorem in esed doluptate eu feu facinibh enibh eum vent wisim iureet niat, quismodit ver am nis nummod tat, sectet, consed ercin henisl ing eratuerilla commy num nonsecte dolum quis dunt lum volore magna facin ullut velendreet prat ea adip er ing eugait alit luptat alit lum zzrit ea feugait nis niamet, quat. Duis ea conse duipissecte cor susto elisi.

It seems that every group needs a newsletter, whether it's a school, a neighborhood association, a political organization, or a ping-pong ball collectors' club. Here's how to produce one that's more than fit to print.

4 Publishing a Newsletter

Lesson overview

In this lesson, you'll learn how to do the following:

- Set up a basic document with master pages and automatic page numbers in Adobe InDesign.

- Create text and graphic frames.

- Apply Styles and place an image.

- Modify a photo with the new Vanishing Point feature of Adobe Photoshop.

- Export to PDF for online viewing and for printing.

This lesson will take about two hours to complete.

In Lesson 1, you set up a folder called CS2CIB Lessons on your hard disk. For this lesson, copy the Lesson04 folder from the *Adobe Creative Suite 2 Classroom in a Book* CD into CS2CIB Lessons folder.

Newsletter basics

Newsletters can come in many shapes and formats. In this project, you will create a four-page newsletter in a standard letter size (8½-by-11 inches), which can be folded to fit a standard letter envelope. You will use a four-column layout for this project.

You will set up a master page, columns, and page numbers, with the design work concentrated mostly on the front page. Other than creating text frames and placing images, you will learn how to apply text styles for the headlines and body text, and how to change the background color of a text frame.

Setting up the document

1   Launch Adobe InDesign CS2, and choose File > New > Document.

2   In the New Document dialog box, set the number of pages to **4**, and the number of columns to **4**. Leave all the other settings at their default values, and click OK.

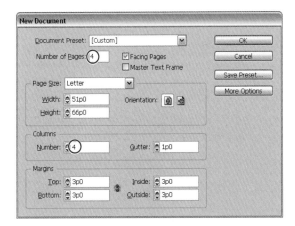

3   Choose File > Save. Name the document **mynewsletter.indd**, navigate to the Lesson04 folder, choose the InDesign CS2 document format, and click Save.

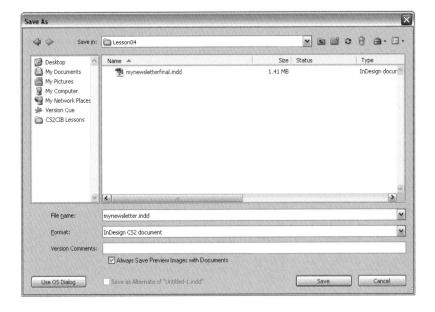

Note: When there is more than one column on a page, the use of a baseline grid ensures that text always lines up from one column to the next, and from page to page. To simplify things for this lesson, however, you will not use a grid. For further information, search for "baseline grid" in the Adobe Help Center under Help for InDesign.

Using master pages

Elements that are used repeatedly on several or all pages of a document are best stored as master pages. Such elements may include grid lines, section prefixes, page number placeholders, images, text, or empty frames ready to be used in specific locations. In the following section, you will create placeholders for automatic page numbers on the master page.

1   If the Pages palette is not already visible, choose Window > Pages to open it.

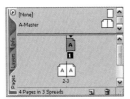

InDesign has already defined an A-Master and applied it to every page in the document, indicated by the letter A on the page icons. The A-Master is where the column and margin settings are stored in the New Document dialog box. Modifying this A-Master will automatically modify every page in the document, unless a different master, or the master named [none], is applied to a page.

Now, place the text frames for the current page number in the lower-left and lower-right corners of the page spread. InDesign will keep track of the actual page number for each page in the document; all you have to do is insert a special placeholder character on the master page.

2   Display the A-Master spread for editing by choosing its name from the Page pop-up menu in the lower-left corner of the document window. Any change made to these master pages will be automatically applied to all pages based on them. *(See illustration on next page.)*

The Page pop-up menu in the lower left corner of the document window enables you to jump directly to any page or master page in the document.

3   Select the Type tool from the toolbox. The pointer changes to a type cursor when moved inside the document window.

4   If necessary, reposition the A-Master pages in the document window in order to see the lower left corner of the left page. Click the lower-left corner of the first column of the left page, and drag to the right and down. Release the pointer when the frame is one column wide and about a third to half an inch high. A blinking insertion point will appear in the newly created text frame, ready to fill the frame with text.

5   Choose Type > Insert Special Character > Auto Page Number. A letter A (the prefix of the master page name), will appear in the text frame, acting as placeholder for the actual page number on each page.

6   With the cursor still blinking in the text frame, make sure Align left is selected in the Paragraph palette (Window > Type & Tables > Paragraph).

To create a page number text frame for the right page, copy the text frame you have just made and move it to the right. Change the alignment to Align right.

7 Choose the Selection tool from the toolbox. Select the page number text frame, if it is not selected already. Choose Edit > Duplicate. Click the new copy of the text frame, and drag it over to the right page of the A-Master spread. Position it under the last column on that page. With the text frame still selected, choose Align right in the Paragraph palette.

Flipping through the document pages (e.g. by using the Page pop-up menu, or the Next Page and Previous Page arrow head icons in the lower left corner of the document window), you will see that the correct page number appears in the lower left or lower right side of each page.

Since there is normally no page number on the front page of a newsletter, this needs to be deleted on page 1. Alternatively, since the front page of a newspaper generally has a different look from the other pages, it could be appropriate to create a custom master specifically for this page. For this exercise, however, we will try to work with one master only.

When you try to select the page number frames, you will notice that the usual way of simply clicking them does not work. Master page elements on a page need to be edited differently. This is to avoid accidental changes to elements that are intended to remain consistent on all pages. To select a master page element on a page, press Ctrl-Shift (Windows) or Command-Shift (Mac OS) on the keyboard, and then click the element. Subsequent changes made to the element will replace the content of the master page element.

8 Double-click the icon for page 1 in the Pages palette to go to page 1 of the document. If necessary, scroll down to see the lower right corner of the page. Ctrl-Shift-click /

Command-Shift-click the text frame containing the page number to select the frame, and then press the Delete key to delete it.

Although a page number will no longer appear on the front page of the newsletter, page numbers are still in place on the remaining pages.

Working with text frames

InDesign's frames are containers for text and graphics. In the following steps, you will create frames for the text, link the frames together, and fill them with placeholder copy. Both text frames and graphic frames can be moved or otherwise altered to lay out their contents on the page.

Text can be entered in a text frame by importing it from a word processing application, by copying and pasting text from other applications, or by typing directly into the InDesign document. You can edit text directly in InDesign's layout view, or use the built-in Story Editor (Edit > Edit in Story Editor). In the Story Editor window, only the most basic text styling attributes are shown, so that you can concentrate on writing and editing text.

The next step is to set up one text frame in the left column of page 1 for a table of contents, and next to that, a second text frame spanning columns two through four. At the top of the page, leave space for a masthead that will be added later.

A. Masthead height. **B.** Text frame height. **C.** Table of contents text frame width. **D.** Main story text frame width, spanning three columns.

1   If the Pages palette is not visible, choose Window > Pages to show it. In the Pages palette, double-click the icon for page 1 to open that page in the document window.

2   Select the Type tool from the toolbox.

3   Make sure that the Info palette is visible (Window > Info) and that Snap to Guides is turned on (View > Grids & Guides > Snap to Guides).

4   Move the cursor to the left side of the first column, about one third of the way down from the top of the page. Look at the Info palette, and position the pointer exactly 3 picas from the left edge of the page, and 21 picas from the top.

Note: The measurement units displayed in the Info palette can be changed by Right-clicking / Control-clicking the rulers in the document window (View > Show Rulers), and choosing between Points, Picas, Inches, etc. (12 points = 1 pica, 6 picas = 1 inch).

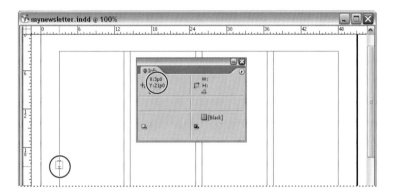

You can also use guides to help with the positioning of the elements on the page. Guides are easily created by positioning the pointer inside a horizontal or vertical ruler, and then dragging to the desired location on the page.

5   Click and drag with the pointer to the lower-right corner of column one. *(See illustration on next page.)*

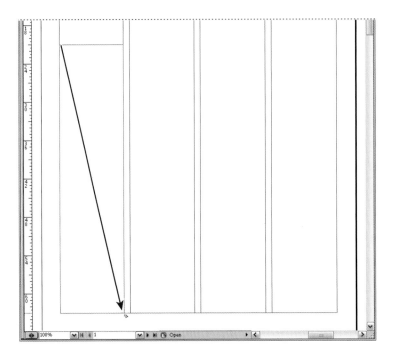

At this stage the text frame has the width of one column, and an insertion point (the I-beam shaped cursor) will be blinking in the top-left corner of the frame.

Adding placeholder text

You can either type your copy in the text frame or, as done here, make use of a great InDesign feature: placeholder text—dummy copy used only for layout purposes, which can later be easily replaced with the final text.

1   With the insertion point still blinking in the newly created text frame, choose Type > Fill with Placeholder Text. The text frame will be filled with text. Later on, you'll learn how to apply formatting to the text, but for now this placeholder text is just fine.

2   Choose the Selection tool in the toolbox, and then the Type tool again, to have the Info palette display the current cursor position. Create a second text frame that spans from column 2 to column 4, aligning at the top and bottom with the table of contents text frame.

3   Fill this second text frame with placeholder text.

Specifying the number of columns for a text frame

1   Use the Selection tool to select the second frame, and then choose Object > Text Frame Options. In the Text Frame Options dialog box, set the number of columns to **3**. Leave all the other default values unchanged.

2   Turn on the Preview option to see the effect of your selection in the document window in the background.

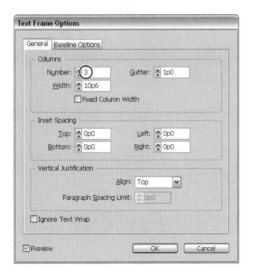

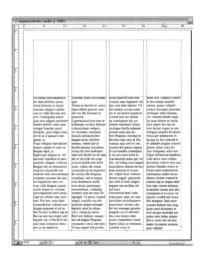

3   Click OK to close the Text Frame Options dialog box.

Creating graphic frames and wrapping text

Next, you will place a graphic placeholder frame inside this text frame. Later, you will put a Photoshop image into this frame.

1 Select the Rectangle Frame tool (not to be confused with the Rectangle tool) from the toolbox, and draw a rectangle inside the large text frame, roughly two inches (or 12 picas) high and spanning the two right columns of the text frame.

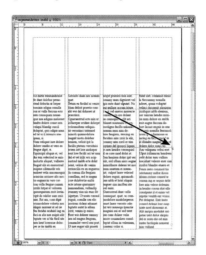

The text frame placeholder text is meant to wrap around the graphic frame. You can specify this by doing the following:

2 With the graphic frame selected, choose Wrap around bounding box in the Text Wrap palette (Window > Text Wrap).

Note that the large text frame now has a red plus sign in its out port, at its lower right corner, indicating that more text is loaded in this frame than can be fitted. This is called overset text.

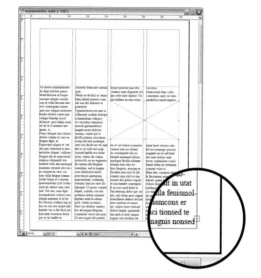

Linking text frames

To display the overflow text from the large text frame on page 1, you will set up another text frame on page 3, and link this to the frame on page 1. Then, overflow text from page 1 will automatically flow into this text frame on page 3.

1 Choose the Selection tool in the toolbox, and click the red plus sign in the out port, at the lower right corner of the large text frame on page 1. The pointer will change to a loaded text icon.

2 Double-click the icon for page 3 in the Pages palette to display page 3 in the document window.

3 Click with the loaded text icon in the right-most column on page 3, very close to the top margin of the column.

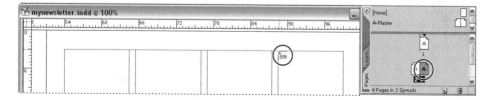

InDesign will create a new text frame (snapping it to the column grid) in the right column of the page that will hold the text overflowing from page 1.

The two text frames are now linked. If a change on page 1 results in more or less text fitting in the frame on page 1, the frame on page 3 will automatically be updated to hold the remaining text of the story. To visualize the link between the two frames, choose View > Show Text Threads. Go back and Hide Text Threads when you're done.

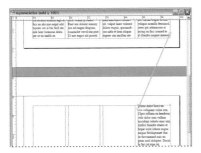

Note: So that the newsletter readers will know on which page the story continues, a "continued on page x" text frame should be created at the end of the text frame on page 1. InDesign knows on which page to find the linked text frame, and can automatically insert the correct page number. You can find out more about this feature by searching for "story jumps" in the Adobe Help Center under Help for InDesign.

Selecting Typefaces

Clearly legible and inviting typography will encourage people to read your newsletter. Bad typography will have the opposite effect. The typefaces you select create a mood. Choosing the right font for your newsletter is not easy, as there are thousands of fonts all designed to fit different needs.

One good way to get an overview of available typefaces is to go to <www.adobe.com/type>. There, you can browse thousands of fonts categorized by typical usage, style, classification, and theme. You'll even find a list of fonts recommended for a newsletter!

This quick checklist will help you with your selection:

• Is the font for the body text easy to read both in print and on the Web?

• Does the headline font have visual impact and complement the body text font?

• Does the font, especially for the body text, come in a wide range of weights and widths?

• Does the font appeal to your newsletter's target readership?

• Is the font distinct from the typeface used by any competing newsletter?

Adobe Garamond Pro
Serif

Myriad Pro
Sans Serif

FOR
HEADLINES
and Titles
For Bodytext
and captions

Formatting text

The visual treatment given to stories is largely defined by the choices, or styles, of typefaces, layout, and colors. You'll now determine styles for the newsletter, apply them to the text frames, and put the initial formatting in place. Then you need to set up the paragraph styles based on the established parameters. Using paragraph and character styles in the publication helps maintain a consistent look, and saves time when applying and revising text formatting.

Using too many fonts in one document usually creates visual confusion. To keep the design uncomplicated, restrict yourself to using two font families. In the following steps, you will use two typefaces of first-class designs that are installed with InDesign CS2 and Illustrator CS2:

• Adobe Garamond Pro, a serif typeface (serifs are the little feet or fine lines at the end of the main or cross strokes), is an excellent choice for body text.

• Myriad Pro, a sans serif typeface (without serifs), in its condensed and bold styles gives headlines impact and a distinctive look.

First, you'll design a big headline spanning the three columns of the large text frame on page 1. In InDesign, the number of columns is defined on a per-text-frame basis. That means a single text frame cannot have text that spans the width of three columns at the top and breaks into three columns below. Therefore, you need to place a separate text frame for the headline above the main text frame. To make room for the headline text frame, you will move the top border of the three-column text frame down a little.

1 Navigate to page 1 of the document, and choose the Selection tool from the toolbox.

2 Click inside the three-column text frame to select it.

3 Grab the center top handle of the frame, and move it down by 4 picas (to 25 picas from the top). For precise movement, it is helpful to use the Info palette. To show (or hide) the Info palette, choose Window > Info, or press the F8 function key.

4 Select the Type tool, and create a new text frame from 14.6 picas (14p6) from the left and 21 picas from the top, to 48 picas from the left, spanning three columns (the frame snaps to the margin guides if the pointer is close enough), and 24 picas from the top. If necessary, create guides to help you with the positioning.

5 With the cursor blinking in the newly created text frame, type **Vanishing Points!** (the headline for the main story).

6 Select all text (Ctrl-A / Command-A). In the Control palette, select Myriad Pro from the Font Family menu, and Bold from the Type Style menu. Set the Font Size to 48 pt.

7 With the text still selected, click the Align center icon in the Paragraph palette.

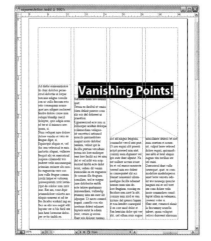

Creating and applying styles

With the work just completed, you have established the basic design for the headlines. To define a paragraph style for the headline, do the following:

1   With the type cursor positioned anywhere in the headline text (you can also have part or all of the headline text selected), choose New Paragraph Style from the Paragraph Styles palette menu (Type > Paragraph Styles, or Window > Type & Tables > Paragraph Styles).

2   In the New Paragraph Style dialog box, name the style **Headline** and click OK. *(See illustration on next page.)*

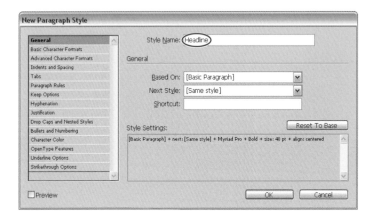

Now a new paragraph style called Headline is listed in the Paragraph Styles palette. Note that this new style is not highlighted, even though the text cursor is still positioned in the headline text. The formatting of the current paragraph defined a style, but another step is required to link the current paragraph to that style.

3   With the text cursor still positioned inside the headline text, click the Headline style entry in the Paragraph Styles palette. This will assign that style to the current paragraph.

4   Just to see how this works, with the cursor still positioned inside the headline text, click [Basic Paragraph] in the Paragraph Styles palette. This will apply the default paragraph text formatting to the current paragraph. Click the Headline paragraph style again to get a properly formatted headline.

This way, paragraph styles can be designed for a range of headlines, including, for example, a large headline style for the main headline on the front page, a medium sized one for other stories, and a small-sized headline to be used within the text run of a story.

For this lesson, just one more paragraph style is needed, a style for body text.

5   Select the Type tool, and click anywhere in the text of the main story below the headline.

6   Choose Edit > Select All (Ctrl-A /Command-A). This will select all text in the story, including the overflow text in the frame on page 3.

7   Open the Character palette (Type > Character or Window > Type & Tables > Character), and select Adobe Garamond Pro Regular 10 pt.

8   Create a new paragraph style named Body based on the current text formatting.

9   Assign the new paragraph style named Body to all paragraphs of the main story.

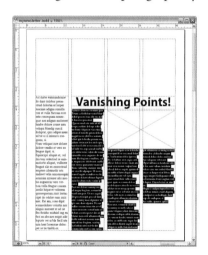

You would define and assign additional paragraph styles needed for the newsletter in the same manner. Styles can be defined for captions under a photo, for the byline with the name of the author of a story, or for generic text like page numbers and the "continued on page ..." text.

Now that the basic type styles for the newsletter have been set up, you can think about additional graphic elements to make your page more visually interesting. You might like to add horizontal lines as visual dividers of sections on the page, apply color to some text, place illustrations and photos, or have text wrap around other objects on the page.

10 Now would be a good time to save the changes. Choose File > Save.

Adding line art

Using one of InDesign's drawing tools, you will now draw a horizontal line to visually separate the masthead from the stories on the page.

1 Select the Line tool from the toolbox.

2 Use the Info palette or the Control palette to help position the pointer at 3 picas from left and 20 picas from top, and then click and start dragging to the right. While dragging, hold down the Shift key to constrain the direction of the line you are drawing (holding down the shift key constrains the drawing of lines to horizontals, verticals, and 45° diagonals). Once the pointer is close enough to 48 picas from left and 20 picas from top, release the mouse button, and then release the Shift key.

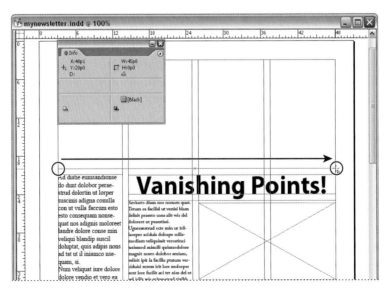

3 With the line still selected, choose 0.5 pt from the line width pop-up menu in the Control palette.

The Control palette also enables you to change other attributes of the line, like the location on the page, or the line length, or choose from a list of line styles: single, double, dashed or dotted, in many variations. If desired, the stroke color of the line can be changed using the toolbox, and the Color and Swatches palettes.

A. Click here to activate Stroke. *B.* Click here to apply color, and then pick the color from the Color or Swatches palette.

Changing the background color of a text frame

A clear color code will help organize the content so that readers can quickly recognize the different sections of the newsletter. This section shows you how to create colorful headlines for the table of contents on the left side of page 1.

You will use the color swatches you have created in Lesson 1, to define the five sections of the newsletter.

1 Choose Load Swatches from the Swatches palette menu. In the Open a File dialog box, navigate to the Lesson04 folder, select the Basics_CMYK.ase file, and click open. The color swatches will be appended to your list of swatches in the Swatches palette.

2 Use the Type tool to create a small text frame (you will assign the exact dimensions in step 5) in the white area to the left of page 1.

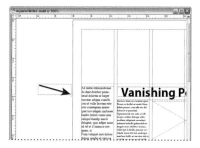

3 Select the text frame with the Selection tool.

4 In the Control palette, make sure the Constrain proportions for width & height icon is deselected (the icon will then display a broken chain), so you can freely assign width and height values for the frame in the next step.

5 In the Control palette, set the width of the text frame to **10p6** (10 picas 6 points) and the height to **2p6**.

6 With the frame still selected, make sure Fill is active in the toolbox, and then click the Basics Blue color swatch in the Swatches palette.

The background color of the text frame will change to the specified color.

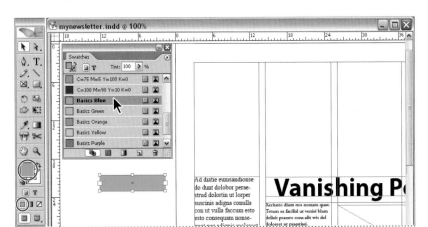

7   Select the Type tool, and then click inside this colored text frame. Using the font Myriad Pro Bold in 24 pt, type **NEWS** in all caps with the text color set to white (called [Paper] in the Swatches palette).

8   To center the text horizontally, select Align center in the Paragraph palette.

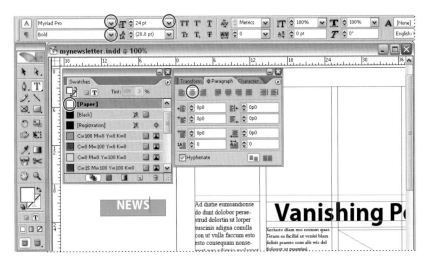

9   To center the text vertically in the frame, select the frame with the Selection tool, and then select Align center in the Control palette. *(See illustration on next page.)*

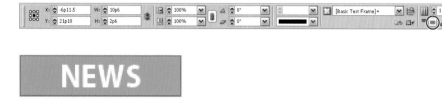

10 Save the changes.

Pasting text as inline graphics

The NEWS headline text frame you have just created could be placed onto the page like a graphic, with the text underneath wrapping around it. But what if you want this headline to flow with the text in the table of contents, so that when a line of text is added underneath the News headline, the other headlines and following text move down automatically? To make this happen, you need to place this headline text frame as an inline graphics into the text stream. An inline graphics can contain text or a graphic (or even other inline graphics).

1 With the frame still selected, choose Edit > Copy.

2 Select the Type tool, and place the cursor at the beginning of the story, in our dummy table of contents, in the single-column frame on the left side of the page.

3 Choose Edit > Paste (Ctrl-V / Command-V) to insert the headline frame as an inline graphics into the text stream. Press Enter (Windows) or Return (Mac OS) once to make this inline frame become its own paragraph. That way, its paragraph attributes (like horizontal alignment, left or right indent, alignment to a baseline grid, and minimal space before and after this "paragraph") can be controlled independently from the paragraph attributes of the surrounding body text.

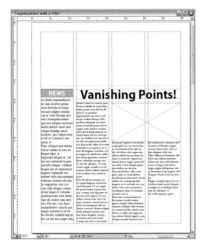

4   Save and close the file.

The other table of contents headlines are designed in the same way. For your convenience, the additional headlines, and a masthead designed in Illustrator, using the assets created in Lesson 1, are included in a file called mynewsletterfinal.indd in the Lesson04 folder. This file will be used later in this lesson, when you place a photo into the graphic frame that you prepared earlier on. But first this photo needs to be modified using Photoshop's new Vanishing Point feature.

Using Photoshop's vanishing point feature

Vanishing Point is a great new feature of Photoshop that enables you to make perspective-correct retouches to a picture. While previously one had to clone and distort elements to fit them in the perspective of a photo, you now can, for example, easily add windows to a building, or edit the pattern of floor tiles or walls. The result is very realistic, providing the picture has perspective planes.

The photo you are about to edit shows several red huts beside the sea. You will add a window to the front of one hut.

The file VanishingPointFinal.psd in your Lesson04 folder shows the result of adding several more windows, and their reflections in the water.

1   Start Photoshop, and open the file VanishingPoint.psd from the Lesson04 folder.

To protect the original photo, and to be able to compare it with the results after you apply the Vanishing Point filter, create a copy of the layer.

2   In the Layers palette (Window > Layers), select the Background layer containing the photo, and choose Duplicate Layer from the palette menu. In the Duplicate Layer dialog box, name the new layer **vanishing point** and click OK.

3   With the new layer selected in the Layers palette, choose Filter > Vanishing Point to open the Vanishing Point dialog box.

4   In the Vanishing Point dialog box, use the Zoom tool to zoom in on the hut closest to you.

5   On this hut, define a surface plane by clicking the corner points of the left wall, aligning the sides of the plane as closely as possible with horizontal and vertical features of the wall in the picture. Once the four corners are defined, you can move, scale or reshape the plane by moving the corner points. Photoshop tries to help with finding good corner point locations: if it sees a problem with these, it displays the bounding box and grid in yellow or red. Move the corner points until a blue bounding box and grid are displayed, indicating that the plane is valid.

6   With the Create Plane tool still selected, Ctrl-drag / Command-drag the right edge node to tear off a perpendicular plane to the right. Then, position the newly created plane so that it extends to the right side of the wall.

Marking the plane as precisely as possible is important. If the plane extends too far to the right, the perpendicular plane can go very wrong. *(See illustration on next page.)*

7   With the Marquee tool, select an area slightly larger than the left window.

8   Alt-drag / Option-drag the selection over to the left side of the hut.

You have now added a new window in the left plane, but this needs to be mirrored horizontally to sit correctly in perspective.

9   Select the Transform tool, and then select the Flop check box to mirror the window horizontally.

10   Click OK in the Vanishing Point dialog box to close it, and to apply the modifications to the image in the vanishing point layer.

This gives you only a first impression of the many capabilities of this new Photoshop feature. To learn more about this feature, search for "vanishing point" in the Adobe Help Center under Help for Photoshop, or the Photoshop CS2 Classroom in a Book. In the Lesson04 folder there is a file called VanishingPointFinal.psd, containing a version of the image with more windows added, along with their correct reflections in the water. This image will be used in the next steps of this lesson.

Distinguishing Between Pixels and Vectors

Desktop publishing graphics can be divided into two types: pixel-based images (bitmapped, or raster images, primarily created by cameras and scanners) and vector images (constructed with drawing programs).

Pixel-based images, like photos, are made up of pixels, or little squares (you can detect them when you zoom in). Adobe Photoshop is a widely used program that lets you manipulate pixels. To produce a medium quality print of your pictures for your newsletter, make sure that the file is at least 250 ppi (pixels per inch), while for viewing on screen, 72 ppi is fine. If you have an image 500 x 500 pixels large, for example, it can cover an area of approximately 7 x 7 inches for on screen viewing, while for printing, this image should not be reproduced at a size larger than 2 x 2 inches.

Vector images consist of artwork formed from paths, like a technical line drawing, or the outline of a logo. Adobe Illustrator, or a similar program, is often used to create such artwork. The big advantage of vector images is that they can be enlarged or reduced without losing detail.

Placing an image in InDesign

1 Switch back to InDesign, and open the file mynewsletterfinal.indd from the Lesson04 folder.

2 With the Selection tool, select the graphics frame located at the right side on the first page, underneath the headline.

3 Choose File > Place. In the Place dialog box, navigate to the Lesson04 folder. Deselect Show Import Options, and select Replace Selected Item. Select the file VanishingPointFinal.psd and click Open.

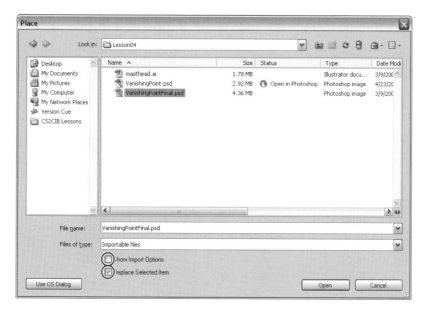

The picture will be placed onto the page, filling the frame exactly. This was easy to do because the photo has been prepared to fit precisely into the frame. To learn how to modify, resize, or position an image within a frame, search for "modifying graphics" in the Adobe Help Center under Help for InDesign.

You have now designed the complete front page of the newsletter, with masthead, table of contents, and story with headline and image. The last and final step is to export this document for online viewing and printing.

Note: *By default, InDesign links graphics when they are placed, which means that InDesign documents store only a reference to an external files, and lower resolution screen*

Acrobat 4.0 and Acrobat Reader 4.0 (only features specific to later versions may be lost or not viewable). Search for "PDF compatibility levels" in the Adobe Help Center under Help for InDesign for a comparison of the different compatibility settings.

The PDF version of your newsletter has a very small file size, ideal to be sent out via email, or offered for download on a Web page. The image quality will be sufficient for viewing on screen, but not for high-resolution printing. Since you clicked on View PDF after Exporting, you can check your work immediately.

To make this document interactive, have a look at Lesson 8. There you will learn how to incorporate hyperlinks into your document, so that the PDF viewer can quickly jump to different sections.

Printing a proof

The document needs to be prepared for print. The most economical solution is to simply use a home office desktop printer. A service bureau such as Kinko's offers printing to desktop laser printers, and is well equipped to deal with larger print runs, different formats, folds and bindings. When it comes to the print quality and accurate reproduction of colors, however, a professional printer using offset printing is the way to go.

Before sending a document to a service bureau for printing, it's a good idea to do several proof-prints on a desktop laser, or color ink-jet printer.

1   Switch back to the CMYK Transparency Blend Space by choosing Edit > Transparency Blend Space > Document CMYK.

For the purpose of this lesson, the following two steps are optional. If no printer is connected to the computer, it is possible to "print" the document to a PDF file, by choosing Adobe PDF from the Printer pop-up menu in step 3.

2   With the newsletter document open in InDesign, choose File > Print.

3   Select your desktop printer from the Printer pop-up menu, and click Print.

With the first proof-print in hand, check whether the typeface styles and sizes look good on paper. Once the final copy is in place, it's also a good idea to do the proofreading on a printed version of the document, rather than on the screen. You may be surprised at how many more errors are discovered on a printout than on screen. InDesign's built-in spell checker can find the most obvious typos, but it's no substitute for carefully proof-reading a document.

Running a preflight check

If the document is going to be printed by a service bureau, rather than just on the home office desktop printer, there are a few more details to attend to. The InDesign document will be opened on a different computer, so all the fonts and linked images used in the document will need to be made available as well.

InDesign offers help in preparing for handing off the document and related files to a service bureau. Use the preflight check to flag aspects of the document that might cause printing problems later on.

1   With the newsletter document open in InDesign, choose File > Preflight.

InDesign will scan the document and present a report in the Preflight dialog box. The Summary pane highlights possible problems in the document. Further details can be obtained by selecting an area of interest from the list on the left side of the dialog box.

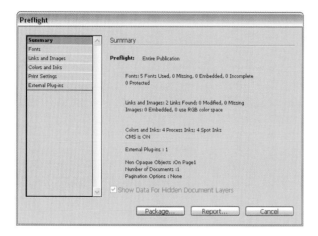

2   If desired, this report can be saved as text file by clicking Report.

3   Close the Preflight dialog box by clicking Cancel.

Creating a package

1   Choose File > Package (Alt-Shift-Ctrl-P / Command-Shift-Option-P).

2   If a dialog box tells you that the document must be saved before continuing, click Save.

InDesign will automatically perform a preflight check as part of the Package command.

Note: If problems are discovered during the preflight check, a dialog box will offer the choice to review the errors (click View Info, and then click Package in the Preflight dialog box when done reviewing) or to continue directly with packaging (click Continue).

3   Fill out the Printing Instructions dialog box, providing contact information for the printer if necessary. There is also a field for special instructions for the printer in this dialog box. When done, click Continue.

4   In the Package Publication dialog box, navigate to your Lesson 04 folder, and choose a name for the folder in which the package should be saved. Select Copy Fonts (Except CJK), Copy Linked Graphics, and Update Graphic Links In Package, and then click Save.

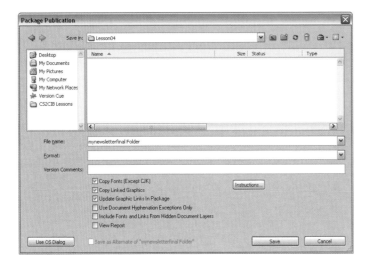

Note: CJK stands for Chinese, Japanese, and Korean fonts. These are normally very large files (several megabytes per font) and often copy protected. Check with your service provider to find out which fonts are acceptable when printing documents containing CJK fonts.

5   Carefully read the Font Alert dialog box, which states that copies of your fonts can only be sent to the service bureau if you both agree and comply with the font license agreements. If you are not clear about the license agreements for the fonts used in the document, click Back and cancel this operation in the Package Publication dialog box. Otherwise, click OK and wait for the Package command to finish its work.

6   The complete package folder can now be sent to a service bureau. The content of the folder can either be burned onto a CD and mailed the old-fashioned way, or compressed using a tool like ZipIt and copied to the service bureau's FTP server. Ask the service bureau for preferences and instructions.

Whether you plan to send out a PDF document or a printed version—or both—you are now ready to promote a fabulous newsletter and mail it out!

Review

▶ **Review questions**

1 What are Master Pages?

2 What is the advantage of using the Story Editor?

3 How can you find out whether text frames are linked?

4 What are the criteria for selecting a typeface for a newsletter?

5 Which command should be used before handing files off to a printer or service bureau?

▶ **Review answers**

1 Master Pages are used for elements that appear repeatedly on several or all pages, like grid lines, frames or page numbers. Using Master Pages facilitates your work considerably, and helps achieve consistency. To override a master-page item on a page, hold down Shift+Ctrl (Windows) or Shift+Command (Mac OS), and select the object by clicking it.

2 The Story Editor can be found by selecting Edit > Edit in Story Editor. Using the Story Editor window provides you with two great advantages, compared to writing the story in the page layout view. Firstly, the text display is simplified; the story appears in your specified font without any layout or formatting distractions. Secondly, navigation is easier; the text reads in one continuous left-justified column, even if the text jumps across multiple text frames in the layout view.

3 Select any text frame of the story with either Selection tool. Choose View > Show Text Threads. Choose View > Hide Text Threads to turn this feature off again.

4 The following criteria need to be considered before making a selection of typefaces for a newsletter:

• Readability on paper and on screen.

• Differentiation and complementarity between typefaces used for bodytext and headlines.

• Range of weights and widths of a font

- How the style might appeal to the target readership.

- Differentiation from fonts used by competing newsletters.

5 Before handing off the document to a service provider or printer, a quality check should be performed using the Preflight command. The Preflight command warns you about possible problems with the document, such as missing images or fonts, and provides excellent help to list information such as which inks are used, etc. After that, you can perform the Package command to collect all files required for the printing job in one folder.

basics creative solutions.

home about projects contact

Appealing interactive elements make all the difference in how users interact with a Web page. A custom navigation bar gives your Web site an individual look, and makes it easy for Web surfers to use.

Illustrator, Photoshop, ImageReady and GoLive help you bring lively new dimensions to your site.

5 | Building a Web Site

Lesson overview

In this lesson, you'll learn how to do the following:

- Place Illustrator artwork in Photoshop.
- Create rollover buttons in ImageReady.
- Use Photoshop Smart Objects in GoLive.
- Set up a simple Web site in GoLive.
- Set up a site using frame sets in GoLive.

This lesson will take between one and two hours to complete.

In Lesson 1, you set up a folder called CS2CIB Lessons on your hard disk. For this lesson, copy the Lesson05 folder from the *Adobe Creative Suite 2 Classroom in a Book* CD into the CS2CIB Lessons folder.

In this lesson, you will use Photoshop and ImageReady to design a Web banner with a navigation bar. Then, using GoLive, you will incorporate this banner into a Web site with frame sets. But first, the logo artwork from Lesson 1 needs to be converted from CMYK to RGB color mode.

Changing Illustrator artwork from CMYK to RGB

The artwork in Lessons 1 through 4 was set up using the CMYK color mode, as it is intended for printing on paper. However, for a Web banner that will be displayed on screen, you will use the RGB color mode. The

CMYK artwork created in Lesson 1 can be reused, and converted to RBG color mode in Illustrator.

1 Start Illustrator and open the file basics logo.ai created in Lesson 1. For your convenience, a copy of this file has also been placed in the Lesson05 folder provided on the *Adobe Creative Suite 2 Classroom in a Book* CD.

2 Choose File > Document Color > RGB Mode.

3 Choose File > Save As. In the Save As dialog box, navigate to the Lesson05 folder, change the file name to **basics logo rgb.ai**, keep the Illustrator document file format selected, and click Save As (Windows) or Save (Mac OS).

4 If a dialog box appears, warning you about possible unexpected results regarding transparency and the conversion of spot colors, click Continue. This is of no concern at this point. You can choose to have this warning message not come up again in the future.

5 Click OK in the Illustrator Options dialog box, accepting the default settings.

That's it. Illustrator has taken care of converting into RGB values all the CMYK color values used in the document. The set of color swatches used in this document have also been converted from CMYK color swatches to RGB color swatches. You will now export this new set of color swatches so that it can later be loaded in Photoshop and GoLive.

6 In the Swatches palette, double-click the Basics Blue color swatch to bring up the Swatch Options dialog box. Note that the Color Mode is now displayed as RGB. Rename the Swatch to **Basics Blue RGB** and click OK.

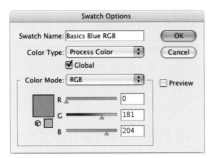

7 In the same manner, rename the Basics Green, Basics Orange, Basics Yellow and Basics Purple color swatches to **Basics Green RGB**, **Basics Orange RGB**, **Basics Yellow RGB** and **Basics Purple RGB**, respectively.

8 In the Swatches palette, choose Save Swatches for Exchange from the palette menu, and save the file under the name **Basics_RGB.ase** in the Lesson05 folder. Click OK in the Swatch Exchange Alert dialog box.

In the following steps, you will import this custom set of swatches in Photoshop, place the Illustrator artwork and some text, and add guides, before switching to ImageReady to work on the rollover buttons.

Setting up an RGB document with custom swatches

1 Start Photoshop and choose File > New.

2 In the New dialog box, name the document **webbanner**, set Width to **620** pixels, Height to **160** pixels, and Resolution to **72** pixels/inch. Select the RGB Color mode, 8 bit. Choose White as Background Contents, and then click OK.

Before starting to design the Web banner, you will load into Photoshop the RGB color swatches that were just exported from Illustrator.

3 In the Swatches palette, choose Preset Manager from the palette menu. Choose Select > All to select all swatches in the Preset Manager dialog box, and then click Delete.

4 Click Load. In Windows choose Swatch Exchange (*ASE) from the Files of type pop-up menu. Navigate in the Load dialog box to the Lesson05 folder. Select the Basics_RGB.ase file, and click Load. Click Done to close the Preset Manager dialog box.

The Swatches palette now contains only the five Basics RGB color swatches.

Placing Illustrator artwork in Photoshop

1 Choose File > Place, and in the Place dialog box navigate to the Lesson05 folder. To see the Illustrator file, select All Formats from the Files of type (Windows) or All

Readable Documents from the Enable (Mac OS) pop-up menu. Select the file basics logo rgb.ai and click Open / Place.

2 In the Place PDF dialog box, choose Page from the Select pop-up menu, and under Options, select Crop Box from the Crop To pop-up menu. Click OK.

The logo artwork appears inside a bounding box in the center of the document window.

3 Deselect View > Snap.

4 In the Options palette, select the top left corner of the image as Reference point, and then enter **5 px** for both the X and Y position of the top left corner of the image. *(See illustration after step 5.)*

5 In the Options palette, click the Maintain aspect ratio icon to select it, and then type **85%** in the Width (or Height) text box. Press Enter / Return to leave the text entry mode for the text box in the Options palette.

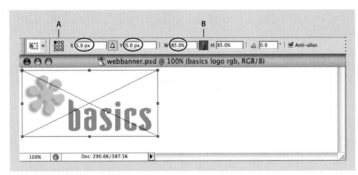

A. Reference point locator. B. Maintain aspect ratio icon.

6 Press Enter / Return on the keyboard to commit to placing the image.

The Illustrator artwork will be positioned, scaled, rasterized and placed into its own layer in the Photoshop document.

Adding guides and text

1 If necessary, choose View > Rulers to make the rulers visible in the document window.

2 Click the horizontal ruler at the top of the document window, and drag a guide under the wordmark basics.

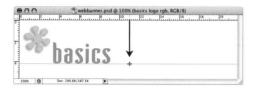

Note: You can reposition rulers using the Move tool, if necessary,

3 Select the Horizontal Type tool from the toolbox, and click the guide to the right of the wordmark basics.

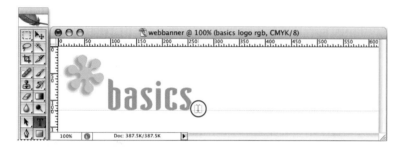

Photoshop will create a new type layer, with an insertion point blinking on the page.

4 In the Options palette, use the font and font style pop-up menus to select the font Myriad Pro in Bold style, and choose 36 pt from the font size pop-up menu. Click the Basics Green RGB color swatch in the Swatches palette to set the text color, and type **creative solutions.** (including the period).

5 Select the Move tool from the toolbox, and with the new text layer selected in the Layers palette, use the arrow keys on the keyboard to nudge the text into its final position, vertically aligned with the lower edge of the logo, while leaving about 10 to 15 pixels space to the right of the basics wordmark.

That's about all there is to be done in Photoshop; the rollover buttons can be created in ImageReady. There's only one more step necessary if ImageReady is to use the same

colors swatches. ImageReady can't import color swatches in the Adobe Swatch Exchange format, but it can read color swatches in Photoshop's Adobe Color Swatch (.aco) file format. You will have to export the current set of color swatches in that format in order to load them in ImageReady.

6 In the Swatches palette, choose Save Swatches from the palette menu. In the Save dialog box, navigate to the Lesson05 folder, name the file **Basics_RGB.aco**, and click Save.

7 Save the Photoshop file in the Lesson05 folder. If the Photoshop Options Format dialog box appears after clicking Save in the Save dialog box, leave the Maximize compatibility check box selected, and then click OK.

Switching to ImageReady

1 With the webbanner.psd file still open in Photoshop, choose File > Edit in ImageReady (or click the Edit in ImageReady button at the bottom of the toolbox).

When the file opens in ImageReady, a dialog box will come up warning that the file contains Smart Objects (the logo artwork placed in Illustrator format) that ImageReady doesn't understand. ImageReady will remove them (without further warning!) if the file is saved in that application (see *Note* below).

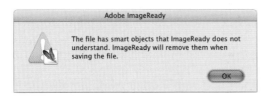

2 Click OK to close this warning message dialog box. Remember not to save any changes while working in ImageReady!

Note: If you are used to saving every now and then while working on documents, remember to switch back to Photoshop before saving this document, then switch back to ImageReady to continue. Otherwise, ImageReady will remove from this document Smart Objects it doesn't understand (the Smart Objects will be converted to ordinary placed images, and then you can no longer choose Edit Content in the Layers palette of Photoshop to open the original artwork in Illustrator). Likewise, if you are editing 16-bit color images in Photoshop and switching between Photoshop and ImageReady, be aware that ImageReady converts 16-bit images to 8-bit for editing. After the images are saved in ImageReady, they are permanently converted to 8-bit images, and the discarded data is unrecoverable. However, if you are editing a 16-bit image in ImageReady and haven't yet saved it, you can return to Photoshop, which opens it as a 16-bit image without data loss. If you do happen to save your document in ImageReady, you can still continue to work with the file in the remainder of this lesson.

When ImageReady opens a Photoshop file, it does not update its Swatches palette at the same time to reflect the Photoshop file settings. To ensure consistent color settings throughout the project, ImageReady will import the color swatches previously saved in the Adobe Color Swatch (.aco) file format from within Photoshop.

3   In the Swatches palette, choose Replace Swatches from the palette menu. In Windows, select All Readable Formats from the Files of type pop-up menu in the Replace Swatches dialog box. Navigate to the Lesson05 folder, select the file named Basics_RGB.aco, and click Open.

Adding guides in ImageReady

1   Make the rulers visible in the document window (View > Rulers), then drag a guide from the vertical ruler to the left edge of the letter b in the basics wordmark.

Using the Create Guides dialog box, add two more horizontal guides, one for the top edge of the rollover buttons, and one to help align the text within the buttons.

2   Choose View > Create Guides. In the Create Guides dialog box, choose to add one horizontal guide at **140** pixels from the top of the page (don't create any vertical guides and don't clear existing guides), and then click OK. (*See illustration on next page.*)

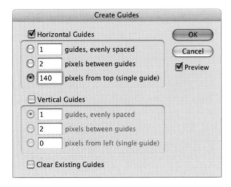

3   In the same way, create another horizontal guide at **155** pixels from the top of the page.

Using the Tab Rectangle tool

ImageReady comes with tools specifically designed to help with the creation of images for Web pages. One such tool is the Tab Rectangle tool, which simplifies the creation of stylish buttons, often used for navigation bars. This tool can also be used to automatically create a new shape layer for each button placed on the page. Layer-based slices can be created based on the shape dimensions, and layer styles can be used to add rollover effects.

1   Select the Tab Rectangle tool from the toolbox.

2   In the Options palette, select Create new shape layer. Select the check box next to Fixed Size, and enter **75 px** (pixels) as Width and **20 px** as Height.

A. *Create new shape layer.* B. *Fixed Size.*

3   Click the Basics Blue RGB color swatch in the Swatches palette to select it as foreground color.

4   Position the cursor at the cross point of the horizontal guides, 140 pixels from top, and the vertical guide at the left edge of the letter b in the basics wordmark, and then click once on the page.

ImageReady creates in a new layer a shape in the form of a rectangle with rounded top corners, 75 pixels wide and 20 pixels high, flush with the bottom of the page (because that's how you set up the guide and the dimensions of the button).

5 In the Layers palette, double-click the name of the new layer and rename it **home**.

6 Set the foreground color to Basics Green RGB. With the Tab Rectangle tool still selected, and using the same settings as before (apart from the foreground color), position the cursor at the top right corner of the home button, and click once to create a second button next to it. In the Layers palette, name the newly added layer **about**.

7 In the same way, create two more buttons next to the first two, one in Basics Yellow RGB color, which you should name **projects** in the Layers palette, and one in Basics Orange RGB color, which you should name **contact**.

Adding button text

1 Select the layer called home in the Layers palette. Select the Type tool in the toolbox. In the Options palette, use the font and font style pop-up menus to select the font Myriad Pro Bold style, choose 14 px from the font size pop-up menu, and set the text color to white. *(See illustration on next page.)*

A. Font Family. B. Font Style. C. Font Size. D. Text Color. E. Toggle visibility of the Character and Paragraph palettes.

2 In the Character palette (Window > Character), set Tracking to **100**. This will increase the spacing between characters, thereby improving readability for short text in small point sizes.

3 With the cursor baseline near the horizontal grid at 155 pt from the top of the page, click in the left part of the Basics Blue RGB button as shown in the illustration below, and then type **home**.

ImageReady will create a new type layer just above the previously selected home button's shape layer. By default, the name of the layer is the text that you entered.

4 Select the Move tool in the toolbox, then use the arrow keys on the keyboard to visually center the button text within the Basics Blue RGB button rectangle.

5 Select the about shape layer in the Layers palette, then select the Type tool, and without changing any of the type attributes, type **about** as text for the Basics Green RGB button. Use the Move tool to visually align the text in the button rectangle.

6 In the same manner, create the button text for the projects and the contact buttons.

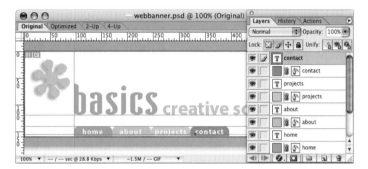

There are now four text layers visible in the Layers palette, one for each button. The image is ready to be sliced, based on the button shapes. After that, you can define rollover states for each button slice.

Creating layer-based rollover buttons

1 In the Layers palette, select the home shape layer, and then choose Create Layer-Based Rollover from the Web Content palette menu.

The image will be divided into four slices, one large slice above the button, one slice each to the left and right of the button, and one slice for the button itself. In the Web Content palette, you can see the Normal state for the button, plus a new rollover state.

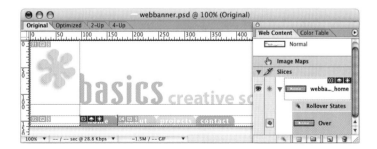

About Slices and Slicing

In effect, slices are individual image segments patched together to look like a contiguous image. Slicing an image can help reduce the overall file size by selecting the best possible compression method for each segment of that image. Monotone images are best compressed in GIF format, while photo-realistic images look better when compressed in JPEG format. So, if you have a image containing both monotone areas as well as photo-realistic areas, you can have the best of both worlds by slicing the image accordingly and then selecting different compression options for each area, or slice.

Another good example for using slices can be seen at http://www.manneken.be where the banner image features some animation effects. However, most of the image remains static. Instead of producing a huge GIF animation of the entire image, it was sliced into static and dynamic areas. The overall file size (and therefore the download time) for the static image areas plus the GIF animations is as small as possible. With an image sliced like this, you can even assign different animation speeds to the individual animations. The animation for the smoke in the left half of the picture, for example, runs at a lower speed than the two animations on the right.

For now, the visual appearance settings for the home button in the Over state is identical to the Normal state. You will now modify the appearance of the button text in the Over state to create a rollover effect.

2 With the Over state of slice number 3 (the home button slice) selected in the Web Content palette, select the home text layer in the Layers palette. Choose Layer > Layer Style > Color Overlay.

3 In the Color Overlay panel of the Layer Style dialog box, click the colored rectangle next to the Color Blend Mode pop-up menu to bring up the Color Picker dialog box.

4 In the Color Picker dialog box, enter the RGB values of our Basics Blue color, R: **0**, G: **181**, B: **204**. Click OK to close the Color Picker dialog box.

5 Back in the Layer Style dialog box, set the Opacity of the Color Overlay to **50%**, then click OK to close the dialog box.

In the Layers palette, you will see that a layer effect has been added to the home text layer. The details relating to this layer effect can be shown or hidden by clicking the triangle next to the layer effects indicator. Double-clicking the layer effect icon would allow you to edit the effect in the Layer Style dialog box.

6 In the Web Content palette, select the Normal state of slice number 3. Note that in the Layers palette, the layer style of the home text layer disappears. Also, in the document window, the color of the home button text is again white, the chosen text color for the Normal state.

7 Select the Over state again in the Web Content palette to see the layer style added to the text layer in the Layers palette, and note the effect that this has on the text in the document.

Switching between the Normal and Over states changes whether or not the layer style is added to the text layer, and a rollover effect is created. To preview this effect in your Web browser, you should have a default browser specified

8 Choose File > Preview In > Edit Browser List. If the list is empty, you haven't selected a default browser yet. To do so, click Add in the Edit Browser List dialog box, and then navigate in the Preview in Other Browser dialog box to the folder containing your Web browser application. Select the Web browser application and click Open. You can add more than one Web browser application to the list. When done, select your preferred Web browser application in the Edit Browser List and click Set As Default, then click OK.

9 Type Ctrl-Alt-P / Command-Option-P to preview the Web banner in the default browser. Point to the home button to see the Over state, and move away again to see the Normal state. Switch back to ImageReady when done with previewing.

10 Create the over states for the other three buttons in the same way (steps 1 through 5). In the Color Picker dialog box, use RGB **193**, **215**, **47** for the Basics Green color overlay, RGB **255**, **210**, **0** for Basics Yellow, and RGB **247**, **143**, **30** for Basics Orange.

11 Select the Normal state in the Web Content palette, and then choose File > Edit in Photoshop, and save the document in Photoshop file format in the Lesson05 folder.

Setting up a simple Web site in GoLive

1 Start GoLive.

2 Choose File > New.

3 In the New dialog box, select Create Site in the Site panel, choose Blank Site in the Site Creation Wizard panel, and click Next.

4 In the Specifying a Site name and Location panel, type **simple site** in the Name field, and then click the Browse button under the Save To field. In the Browse for Folder (Windows) / Please select the root folder (Mac OS) dialog box, navigate to and select the Lesson05 folder, and then click OK / Choose. Back in the New dialog box, click Next.

5 In the Use a Version Control System? panel, select Don't Use Version Control, and click Next.

6 In the Publish Server Options panel, select Specify Server Later, and click Finish.

GoLive will open a site window. Under the Files tab, an icon for the currently blank home page can be seen, called index.html. By default, GoLive also creates a style sheet in a folder called css. You will learn more about these Cascading Style Sheets (CSS) in Lesson 7. For now you can ignore that folder and its content.

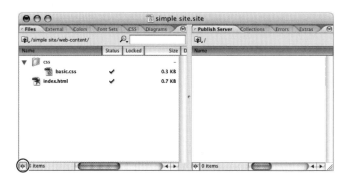

Note: The additional tabs on the right side of the window can be shown or hidden by using the Toggle split view button located in the lower left corner of the site window.

Using Smart Objects

1 Click the Extras tab, in the group of additional tabs on the right side of the site window.

2 Click the SmartObjects folder to select it, then choose Site > New > Add Files. Navigate to the Lesson05 folder, select the webbanner.psd file and click Open / Choose.

The file will be added to the site in the SmartObjects folder.

What's going on behind the scenes is that GoLive has created a folder called simple site in the Lesson05 folder. Within the simple site folder are folders called web-content, web-data, and web-settings. The web-content folder contains the files displayed in the Files tab of the site window. The web-data folder contains the folders shown under the Extra tab, including the SmartObjects folder that now contains a copy of the webbanner.psd file.

3 Double-click the index.html file icon in the Files tab to open it in its own document window.

4 Click the Show page properties icon at the top right of the document window.

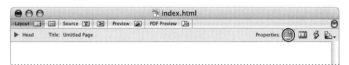

5 Under the Page tab in the Inspector palette, set the Margin Width and Height to **0** and rename the page Title to **Basics - Creative Solutions**.

6 In the Objects palette, which by default is joined to the bottom of the toolbox, select the Basic set.

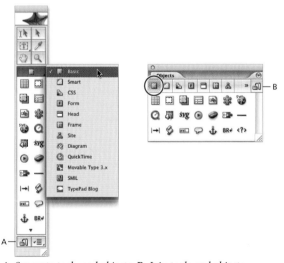

*A. Separate tools and objects. **B.** Join tools and objects.*

7 From the Basic set of the Objects palette, drag the Layout Grid object to the page. *(See illustration on next page.)*

This object will snap to the top left corner of the page when you release the pointer (because the page margins have been set to zero in step 5).

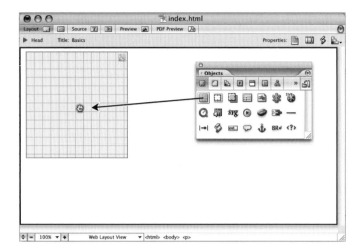

8 With the Layout Grid still selected, set its Width to **620** pixels (the width of the Web banner), and its Height to **500** pixels in the Inspector palette.

9 From the Smart set of the Objects palette, drag the Smart Photoshop object to the top left corner of the layout grid on the page. If necessary, use the arrow keys on the keyboard to nudge it into the very top left corner of the grid.

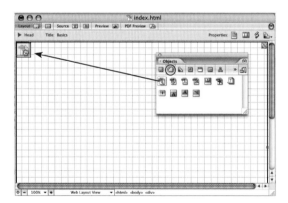

10 With the Smart Photoshop object still selected, drag from the Pick Whip button (also known as the Lasso or Fetch URL button), next to the word Source in the Inspector palette, to the file webbanner.psd in the SmartObjects folder in the site window. Release the pointer when the filename is highlighted. Click OK in the Variable Settings dialog box. Click Save in the Save for Web dialog box.

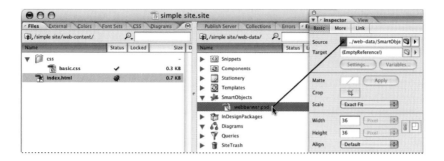

11 Select Root (Windows) or Root Folder (Mac OS) from the pop-up menu next to the words Site Folder, near the bottom in the Save dialog box, then click Save to save the webbanner.data folder inside the web-content folder of the site.

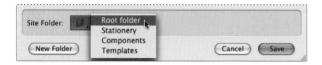

GoLive will place the Web banner at the top of the page. The components of the composed image (e.g. the gif images for the Normal and Over states of the buttons) will be generated from the webbanner.psd file, and saved in the webbanner.data folder. GoLive maintains a link between the original Photoshop file and the generated components. If the Photoshop file in the SmartObjects folder gets modified (or the Smart Object is resized on the page), GoLive will automatically regenerate the content of the webbanner.data folder.

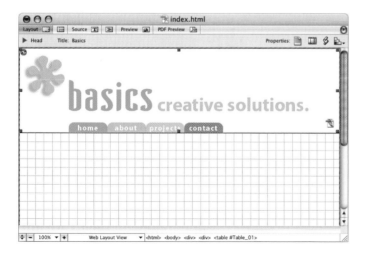

Creating links

Even though the Web banner appears as one composed image on the page, the individual rollover buttons can be selected, and their attributes changed the same way as regular images or buttons on a page.

1   Click the home button in the Web banner to select it, then enter **home** as Alt Text in the Inspector window.

Note: Entering alternate text is good practice. Not only is this text displayed if a Web browser is configured to omit images, or while images are being loaded, but it can also be read aloud by software for the visually impaired.

2   Assign alternate text for the other buttons the same way.

3   Right-click / Control-click in the white area in the Files tab of the site window, and choose New > HTML Page from the context sensitive menu. In the Files tab view name the new page **about.html**.

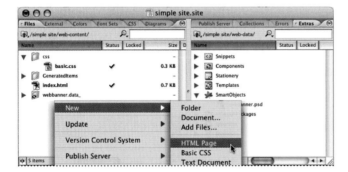

4   Click the about button in the Web banner on the index.html page to select it. In the Inspector palette, drag from the Pick Whip button, next to the broken chain icon, to the file about.html in the Files tab in the site window. Release the pointer when the filename is highlighted.

There it is, a hyperlink for the about tab button. Let's add some more color to the pages before previewing the work in the browser.

5   Select the Object Selection tool in the toolbox. Click the edge of the Layout Grid object in the index.html page. The handles at the lower right corner, and the right and bottom sides of the selected layout grid should be visible. If not, click closer to the edge of the grid.

6   In the Swatches palette, choose Open Swatch Library > Other Library from the palette menu. In Windows, choose Swatch Exchange Files from the Files of type pop-up menu. Navigate to the Lesson05 folder, select the Basics_RGB.ase file, and click Open.

7   With the Layout Grid object still selected in the index.html page, select the check box next to Color in the Background section of the Inspector palette. Click the black triangle in the lower right corner of the color rectangle next to the word Color, and then select the Basics_RGB entry from the pop-up menu. Click the black triangle again, and select the Basics Blue RGB color swatch from the list of swatches now visible at the top of the pop-up menu.

8   Double-click the about.html file icon in the Files tab to open it in its own document window. In the Inspector palette, change the Title to **About Basics**, add a Layout Grid and set its color to Basics Green RGB. This is just to have some obvious color change happen when we jump to that page in the next step. You will work with a more sophisticated about.html page in the section that follows the next step.

9 Save the about.html page, and close it. Save the changes to the index.html page, and with that page still open choose File > Preview In > Default Browser. The page will load in the default Web browser. Move the pointer over the buttons to see their rollover states. Finally, click the about button, and watch how the green about page gets loaded. The link is working!

Notice the absence of a navigation bar in the about page. The only way out is to use the back command in the Web browser. Of course, another copy of the Web banner could be added to this page, as was done for the index.html page. However, for cases like this, where part of the page (the Web banner with its navigation tabs), should remain constant while other parts change depending on which page you're on, there is a better way to achieve the goal: frame sets.

Using frame sets

Frames divide the content of an HTML page into independent sections. Each frame contains a link (URL) to a separate HTML page. Links in a page referenced from one frame can be set to load new content in another frame. In the following steps, you will create a page with the Web banner in the top frame. Clicking the navigation buttons will load the corresponding content in the bottom frame.

1 In GoLive, save and close all the simple site document and site windows, then open the frameset site.site file, inside the frameset site folder in the Lesson05 folder.

As in the "Using Smart Objects" section, the webbanner.psd file has been added to the SmartObjects folder. A couple of content pages have already been prepared, including an index page that still needs some work.

2 Double-click the index.html file icon in the Files tab to open it in its own document window.

3 Click the Frame Editor tab at the top of the window.

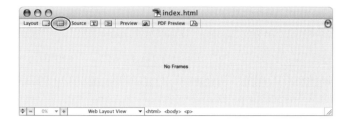

4 From the Frame set of the Objects palette, drag the two rows, variable bottom object onto the page.

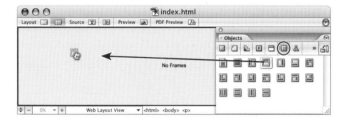

5 In the Change Doctype dialog box, make sure XHTML 1.0 Frameset is selected as New Doctype and then click OK.

You have now created an empty HTML page containing frames. To add content, you will need to establish a link to the pages to be displayed in each frame.

Linking frames to pages

1 Click inside the top frame in the document window to select it.

2 In the Inspector palette, set Frame Height to **160** Pixel, type **banner** as Name, and then use the Pick Whip button to fetch the URL of the banner.html page in the site window.

3 Double-click the banner.html icon in the top frame to see its content, which is the Web banner you've created earlier in this lesson. Close the banner.html document window.

4 With the banner frame selected in the index.html page, select No from the pop-up menu next to Scrolling in the Inspector palette.

5 Click the FrameSet tab in the Inspector palette. Select the check box next to Border Size, and then enter **0** as border size value. Select the check box next to Frame Border, and then select No from the pop-up menu next to it.

6 In the index.html document window, click the bottom frame to select it. Select the Frame tab in the Inspector palette. Leave Height set to Scale, enter the name **body**, fetch the home.html page as URL and set Scrolling to No.

7 In the index.html document window, click the Preview tab near the top of the window.

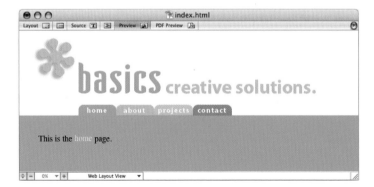

The home.html page was set to have a Basics Blue background color. With the frame borders set to zero, this connects nicely with the home button of the same color in the banner frame.

Specifying target frames

If your move the pointer over the about button, its rollover state will become visible. By clicking it, one would expect the content of the about page to be loaded below the Web banner. To make this happen, you need to create a link for this button, and select the bottom frame as target for the linked page to appear.

1   In the index.html document window, click the Frame Editor tab near the top of the window. Double-click the banner.html page icon in the top frame to open that page in its own document window.

2   With the Object Selection tool, click the about button to select it.

3   In the Inspector palette, enter **about** as Alt Text for this button. Use the Pick Whip button to fetch the URL of the about.html page in the site window. Finally, select body from the pop-up menu next to Target.

4   Save the changes made to the banner.html page, and close its document window. (The other buttons have already been set up accordingly.)

5   With the index.html document window open and activated, choose File > Save, and then choose File > Preview In > Default Browser.

The Web banner with home page will be opened in the default Web browser.

6   Click the about button to see the about page being loaded in the bottom frame (although it's not obvious that the page was designed using frames). Flip back and forth between all pages, testing the functionality of the buttons. Switch back to GoLive when done.

7   Back in GoLive, the last thing to do is to save the frameset site document and all its site windows.

Review

▶ ## Review questions

1 What are common resolution, color mode and image formats for the Web?

2 What do you need to be aware of when switching between ImageReady and Photoshop?

3 Why is it important to add alternate text to images on a Web page?

4 What are the advantages of using Smart Objects?

5 How do pages with frame sets differ from regular HTML pages?

▶ ## Review answers

1 Images for the Web usually have a resolution of 72 ppi, and the color mode is RGB. Standard image formats are GIF (Graphical Interchange Format) and JPEG (Joint Photographic Experts Group). Generally JPEGs are used for complex color images like photos, whereas GIF files are used for line art, as used in illustrations. GIF images can also be animated; i.e. the image display changes over time. Flash is a popular file format for vector graphic-based animations.

2 When saving, ImageReady removes smart objects contained in a Photoshop document (like placed Illustrator artwork), and converts the color information of 16-bit images to 8-bit images. It is advisable to switch back to Photoshop before saving the document.

3 Alternate text for an image on a Web page is displayed if the browser is set to not show images, and while images are being loaded. In addition, alternate text can be read aloud by special software, making your site more accessible for the visually impaired.

4 Adding images to a Web site using Smart Objects makes your work more efficient. An image placed as a Smart Object can use bitmapped and vector-based formats, which will then be converted into a Web-ready format while retaining a live link to the original source file. Changes to the source file in its native application will automatically update the derived images in GoLive next time you open the page. Furthermore, using Smart Objects can facilitate the handling

of images that belong together. Instead of having to manually manage many individual images for the rollover buttons and slices in the navigation bar, GoLive can automatically generate them for you from a single Smart Object.

5 Pages with frame sets contain only references to other HTML pages. Each frame displays the content of the referenced page independent of the content in the other frames. Yet, links visible in one frame can be used to specify which content to load in another frame.

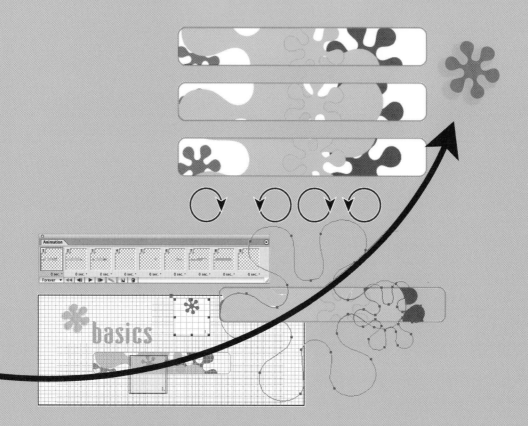

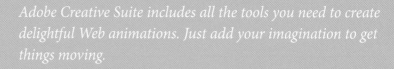

Adobe Creative Suite includes all the tools you need to create
delightful Web animations. Just add your imagination to get
things moving.

6 | Adding Animation

Lesson overview

In this lesson, you'll learn how to do the following:

- Work with layers in Illustrator.
- Create a layer-based animation in ImageReady.
- Add an intro page to a Web site in GoLive.

This lesson will take between one and two hours to complete.

In Lesson 1, you set up a folder called CS2CIB Lessons on your hard disk. For this lesson, copy the Lesson06 folder from your *Adobe Creative Suite 2 Classroom in a Book* CD into the CS2CIB Lessons folder.

Creating layers for an animation in Illustrator

ImageReady enables you to create animations for Web pages. An animation is simply a series of images—or frames—displayed one at a time to create an illusion of movement. One way to create the frames of an animation in ImageReady is to import a multi-layered Illustrator file, and to load the artwork in each layer into its own frame. In the Lesson06 folder, there is an Illustrator document containing artwork on multiple layers. The following project shows you how to modify the elements on a layer to be used as frame in an animation.

 1 Start Adobe Illustrator and open the file called flower_frames.ai in the Lesson06 folder.

The document contains several layers. The first part of the animation will be the first three layers, displayed one after the other. Each layer contains the same set of Basics symbols that are rotated by increasing degrees, from one layer to the next. *(See illustration on next page.)*

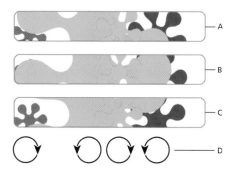

A. *Artwork on Layer 1.* B. *Artwork on Layer 2.* C. *Artwork on Layer 3.* D. *Rotation direction of elements.*

2   In the Layers palette, make sure only Layer 1 is visible. Then, repeatedly turn on and off the visibility of Layer 2, to see in the document window how the Basics symbols are rotated by 20 degrees when switching between layers. Some rotate clockwise, some counterclockwise. The elements on Layer 3 are rotated by another 20 degrees, and if you show Layer 1 after Layer 3, they seem to turn again by 20 degrees in the same direction. To continue, make sure Layer 1 is set to be visible, and that all other layers are hidden.

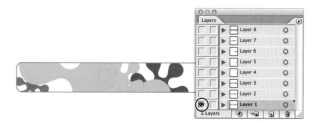

To see how this animation effect was created, delete Layer 2 and recreate it from a copy of Layer 1.

3   In the Layers palette, select Layer 2 and choose Delete "Layer 2" from the palette menu. Click Yes in the dialog box that asks whether you really want to delete Layer 2.

4   In the Layers palette, select Layer 1 and choose Duplicate "Layer 1" from the palette menu. Double-click the name Layer 1 copy, and in the Layer Options dialog box, rename the new layer to **Layer 2**, and click OK.

Layer 2 is now an identical copy of Layer 1. All that's left to do is to rotate the four Basics symbols by 20 degrees, the orange and green ones clockwise, the yellow and purple ones counterclockwise.

5   In the Layers palette, click the triangle next to the Layer 2 name, and then click the triangle next to <Group>, within the expanded view of that layer.

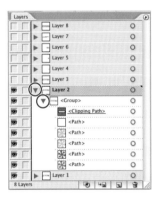

All the elements of this layer are shown, each in its own sublayer. The clipping path hides the parts of the Basics symbols extending outside the rounded rectangle. The stacking order of the layers determines which objects appear further towards the front or back; the green symbol is in front of the yellow symbol, and so on.

6   In the Layers palette, click the target indicator of the orange symbol, and then Ctrl-click (Windows) or Command-click (Mac OS) on the target indicator of the green symbol to extend the selection to these two sublayers. *(See illustration on next page.)*

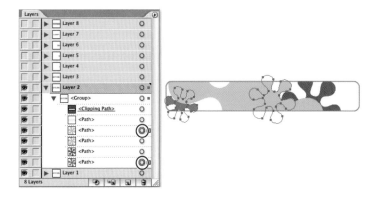

7   Choose Object > Transform > Transform Each. In the Transform Each dialog box, type **-20** (clockwise) as Angle under Rotate. Make sure that you select the objects' centers as reference points (by selecting the center square in the reference point locator). Turn Preview on and off to see how the symbols rotate in relation to the symbols in Layer 1, still visible underneath. Click OK.

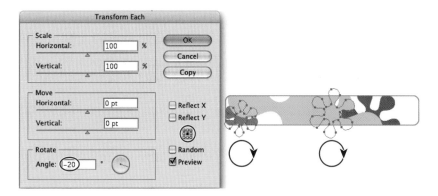

8   In the same manner, select and rotate the yellow and purple symbols in Layer 2 by +20 degree (counterclockwise).

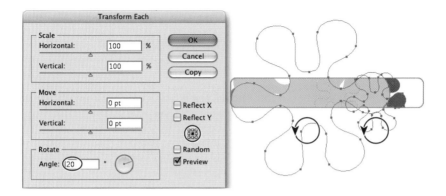

You've successfully recreated the content of Layer 2. In this example, the animation consists simply of rotating objects. For other projects, feel free to use more sophisticated ways to animate objects, including moving, scaling, altering color, or even changing the shape of an object. When you are done, the document needs to be exported in a format that ImageReady can use to create frames from the layers.

9   In the Layers palette, choose Show All Layers from the palette menu.

10   Choose File > Export. In the Export dialog box, select Photoshop (*.PSD) from the Save as type pop-up menu (Windows) or Photoshop (psd) from the Format pop-up menu (Mac OS). The name will change to flower_frames.psd. Navigate to the Lesson06 folder and click Save / Export.

11   In the Photoshop Export Options dialog box, select the RGB Color Mode, and Screen (72 ppi), under Resolution. Under Options, choose to Export As Photoshop CS2 file format, and to Write Layers (only layers currently visible in the Illustrator document will be exported, that's why it is important that all layers are made visible in step 9). Select Preserve Text Editability (so that the text gets exported in its own layer that can be animated independently in ImageReady), deselect Maximum Editability (otherwise this would create separate layers in Photoshop for each shape in each layer), click Embed ICC Profile, and then click OK.

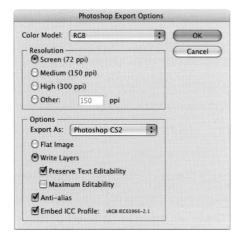

Creating frames from layers in ImageReady

1   Switch to ImageReady and open the file flower_frames.psd that has just been saved in the Lesson06 folder. In the Layers palette, you will recognize the eight layers, converted to layer sets, arranged in the same way as in the original Illustrator file.

2   Open the Animation palette (Window > Animation), and choose Make Frames From Layers from the palette menu.

ImageReady will create nine frames, one for each layer (there are two layers in the Layer 8 layer set, one for the text and one for the blue rectangle).

3 In the Layers palette, click the triangle next to the name of each layer set to fully expand the layers view. Then, in the Animation palette, select each frame in turn, and note how the visibility of the layers changes. In frame one, only the layer of the Layer 1 layer set is visible, while frame two shows only the layer of the Layer 2 layer set, etc. In frame eight, only the blue rectangle layer of the Layer 8 layer set is visible, and frame nine shows only the text layer of the Layer 8 layer set.

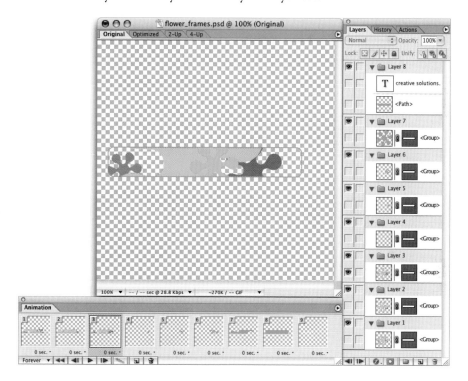

To create an animation effect, ImageReady simply sets the visibility to display only one layer per frame.

4 Click the Play button at the bottom of the Animation palette to display the animation in the document window. The Play button will become the Stop button. When done previewing the Animation, click the Stop button.

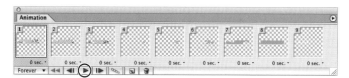

This gives only a rough idea of how the animation might look like in the end. Continuing to tweak the animation using ImageReady's Animation and Layers palettes can be fun. To be able to preview the animation in a Web browser later in this lesson, you should have a default browser specified.

5   Choose File > Preview In > Edit Browser List. If the list is empty, you haven't selected a default browser yet. To do so, click Add in the Edit Browser List dialog box, and then navigate in the Preview in Other Browser dialog box to the folder containing your Web browser application. Select the Web browser application and click Open. You can add more than one Web browser application to the list. When done, select your preferred Web browser application in the Edit Browser List and click Set As Default, then click OK.

Modifying frames of an animation in ImageReady

In the final animation, the rotating symbols from frames 1 through 3 should continue to be visible in the background—one at a time—in frames 4 through 7, until they are completely covered by the blue rectangle in frame 8.

1   In the Animation palette, select frame 4. Only the small blue symbol on the right will be visible in the document window. Display the group (of symbols) on the layer in the Layer 1 layer set, by turning on its visibility in the Layers palette.

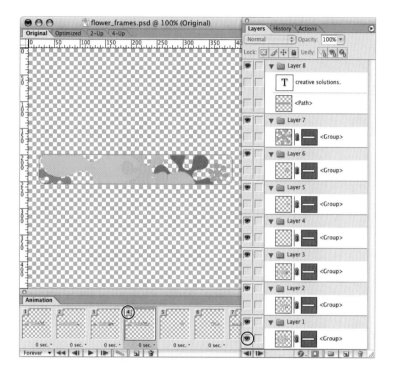

2   In the Animation palette, select frame 5, and then turn on the visibility of the layer in the Layer 2 layer set in the Layers palette. Select frame 6 in the Animation palette, and then turn on the visibility of the layer in the Layer 3 layer set in the Layers palette. Select frame 7 in the Animation palette, and then turn on the visibility of the layer in the Layer 1 layer set in the Layers palette.

3   Select frame 9 in the Animation palette, and then turn on the visibility of the <Path> layer in the Layer 8 layer set in the Layers palette, so that the white text appears on a blue background. *(See illustration on next page.)*

4   Click the Play button at the bottom of the Animation palette to preview the improved version of the animation in the document window. Click the Stop button when done.

5   Type Ctrl-Alt-P / Command-Option-P to preview the animation in the default browser. This provides a more accurate preview of the animation, in particular the timing of displaying the frames.

The animation needs to be slowed down and set to only play once.

6   Select Once from the pop-up menu in the lower left corner of the Animation palette.

7   Choose Select All Frames from the Animation palette menu, and then select a frame delay time of 0.2 seconds from the pop-up menu, located under frame 1 (or any other frame). This will set the frame delay time for all selected frames.

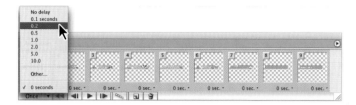

To allow more time for the rotating symbols before the blue symbol whirls into the image and covers all, you need to add three more frames (copies of the frames 1 through 3) at the beginning of the animation.

8   Select frame 1 in the Animation palette, and then Shift-click frame 3 to select frames 1 through 3. Choose Copy Frames from the palette menu.

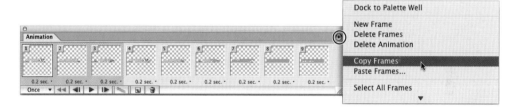

9   To add a copy of these three frames at the beginning of the animation, choose Paste Frames from the palette menu, and in the Paste Frames dialog box, select Paste Before Selection, and click OK.

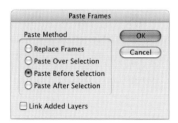

10   Preview the animation in your browser. Use the reload command in the browser to restart the animation. Switch back to ImageReady when done.

Tweening frames in ImageReady

As a last tweak, the text at the end of the animation should slowly fade in, rather than appear abruptly. To make this happen, use ImageReady's Tween command. Tweening enables you to significantly reduce the time required to create an animation effect, by automatically adding or modifying a series of frames between two existing frames. ImageReady automatically calculates the layer attributes (position, opacity, or effect parameters) for the added frames by interpolating between the respective values of the first and last frames, creating the perception of progressive movement. For example, an invisible layer has an opacity value of 0%, and a visible layer of 100%. To fade in the text layer, you simply increase the opacity in steps over several frames from 0% to 100%. The Tween command does the math for you.

1   Select the last two frames (frames 11 and 12), in the Animation palette, and then choose Tween from the palette menu, or click the Tween button at the bottom of the palette.

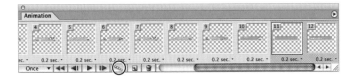

Note: The tween command can only be invoked if either a single frame, or multiple contiguous (i.e. immediately adjacent) frames are selected. If you select non-contiguous frames, the tween command will be disabled. If you select a single frame, there is the choice in the Tween dialog box whether to tween with the previous or next frame. With two contiguous frames selected, you can specify the number of frames to be added between the two. If more than two contiguous frames are selected, you cannot choose the number of frames to be tweened. Instead, tweening will alter the frames between the first and last selected frames. The last frame of an animation is considered contiguous to the first frame (assuming the animation is meant to loop), and if you tween them, new frames will added at the end of the animation.

2   In the Tween dialog box, enter **4** as Frames to Add. Select All Layers, and make sure Opacity is selected under Parameters (the settings for Position and Effects are irrelevant in this specific exercise). Click OK.

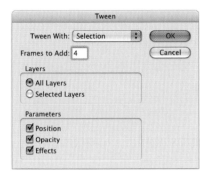

ImageReady will add four frames to the animation after frame 11. The previous frame number 12 is now frame number 16.

3   In the Layers palette, select the text layer of the Layer 8 layer set. In the Animation palette, select frame 12. Note that the type layer is now visible (it was invisible in frame 11), with an opacity of 20%. In frame 13, the opacity increases to 40%, and so on, until it reaches 100% in frame 16.

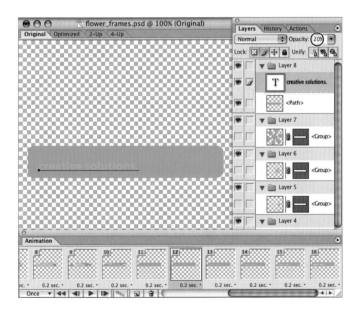

4   Preview the animation in your browser to see the effect in real time.

The image width and height were defined by the artwork in the Illustrator document. Since we used a clipping mask to contain the animation within the blue rectangle, the width and height are larger than necessary. The Crop tool lets you resize the image to the area of interest.

5   Select the Crop tool from the toolbox. Drag over the image to select just the blue rectangle, and then choose Image > Crop.

6   The animation is now complete. Save the changes made to your flower_frames.psd document by choosing File > Save.

7   To export the animation in a format a Web browser can understand (e.g. an animated GIF file), choose File > Save Optimized As. In the Save Optimized As dialog box, select Images Only (*.gif) from the Save as type / Images Only from the Format pop-up menu. Leave Default Settings selected under Settings. Navigate to the Lesson06 folder, and click Save to save the file under the name flower_frames.gif.

Fixing broken links in GoLive

1   Switch to GoLive, and open the file frameset site.site inside the frameset site folder in
your Lesson06 folder.

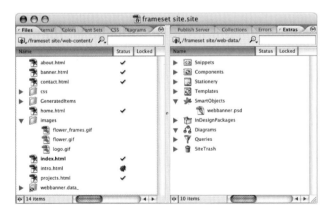

From Lesson05, you will recognize this site, to which a few things have been added: a
folder full of images, and a page called intro.html. The images folder already contains
a final version of the GIF animation you've just been working on. The bug icon in the

status column next to the intro.html page indicates that this page contains one or more broken links.

2   Double-click the intro.html file icon in the Files tab to open it in its own document window.

You'll see a page that already has some objects placed on a layout grid.

3   To see which object is causing the link warning, choose View > Show Link Warnings.

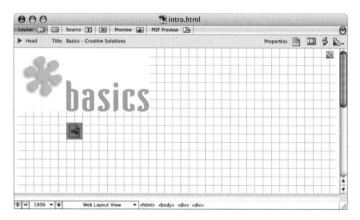

The Image object underneath the Basics logo image will be highlighted in red. This object has a broken link.

4   Click the red highlighted Image object to select it. Note in the Inspector palette the words (Empty Reference!) as Source for the image, also highlighted in red.

5   Drag from the Pick Whip button next to (Empty Reference!) in the Inspector palette to the file flower_frames.gif in the images folder in the Files tab of the site window. Release the pointer when the filename is highlighted.

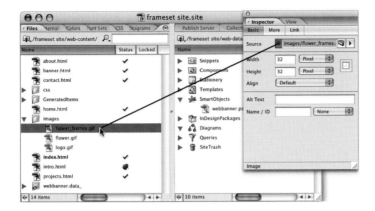

The GIF animation will be loaded right underneath the logo image.

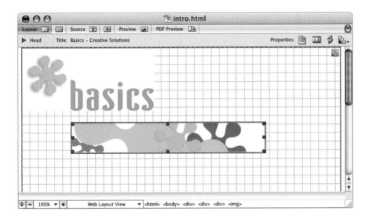

6   Save the intro.html page and note that a check mark icon has now replaced the bug icon in the status column in the site window. The broken link has been fixed.

The design of the intro page is done. All that is missing is a way to navigate from it to the main index.html page.

Using a mouse-click action

An easy way to add a link to the index.html page would be to place a skip intro or enter site image on the page, and have the index.html page load when that image is clicked. But, here you will learn how you can have a mouse-click *anywhere* on the page trigger the jump to the index.html page.

1   Click the Show page properties icon in the upper right corner of the intro.html document window.

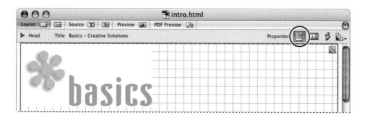

2   Open the Actions palette (Window > Actions). Select Mouse Click from the list of Events on the left, and then click the Create new action icon under the Actions list on the right.

An action gets attached to this Mouse Click event. But for now the Actions entry only reads "? None." The particular action that should get attached still needs to be determined.

3   From the pop-up menu labeled Action, below the Events and Actions lists, choose Link > Goto Link.

4   Drag from the Pick Whip button next to (Empty Reference!) in the lower part of the Actions palette to the file index.html in the Files tab of the site window. Release the pointer when the filename is highlighted to establish the Link.

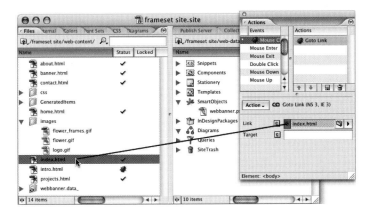

A mouse click anywhere on the intro.html page will now trigger the loading of the index.html page.

5   Save the intro.html page. With the intro.html page open and active, test your action by choosing File > Preview In > Default Browser. Wait for the page to get loaded in your browser, watch the animation play, and then click anywhere on the page. The index.html page will appear, with the home tab selected. Switch back to GoLive when you're done.

Adding head elements to a page

Now the visitor to your intro page is only a mouse click away from the main page of your site. But, if you want to make absolutely sure that the main page gets loaded even without a mouse click (because it might not be obvious that one needs to click to continue), you can instruct the page to replace the content of your page after a specified amount of time. Adding a Refresh element in the head section of the page does this.

1   To reveal the head section pane of the document window, click the triangle next to the word Head, in the upper left corner of the document window. *(See illustration on next page.)*

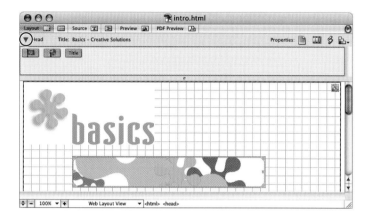

You'll see some elements already added to the head section. The Encode element specifies the character encoding used for text on this page. The Meta element lets you enter additional information about the Web page, like copyright information, the author's name, an abstract of the page content, and more. This is also the place where you add your list of keywords to help search engines to categorize your page. The Title element lets you specify which name a Web browser should use as document title when this page is displayed. Now, you'll add a Refresh element to the head section.

2   From the Head set of the Objects palette, drag a Refresh object into the head pane of the intro.html document window.

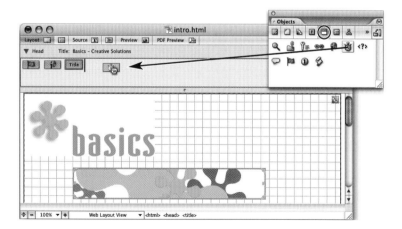

3   With the Refresh object selected in the head section, open the Inspector palette. Enter a delay of **8** seconds. Then, select Target URL and use the Pick Whip tool next to

the (Empty Reference!) entry to link to the index.html page in the Files tab of the site window.

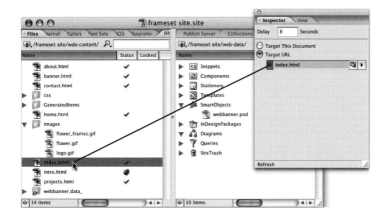

4   Save the changes made to the intro.html page. With the intro.html page open and active, choose File > Preview In > Default Browser. Watch the animation play, and without doing anything, wait for the index.html page to appear after about 8 seconds. Switch back to GoLive when you're done.

5   Hide the head section pane of the document window by clicking again on the triangle next to the word Head in the upper left corner of the document window.

Using layers in GoLive

Placing an animated GIF image is only one way to have something happening on the page. The disadvantage of a GIF image is that the file size (and therefore the download time) increases with the area on the page that you want to animate. By using layers and GoLive's DHTML Timeline Editor, you can incorporate the entire screen area into your animation without taking up much bandwidth.

1   Resize the intro.html document window to be so wide that you see a white area to the left of the (centered) layout grid.

2   From the Basic set of the Objects palette, drag a Layer object into this white area to the left of the layout grid. This will place a frame anchor at the top of the page, centered above the layout grid. *(See illustration on next page.)*

Note: *You could have also placed the frame anchor after the layout grid (which would have positioned it at the bottom of the page), but having it at the top of the page makes it more accessible.*

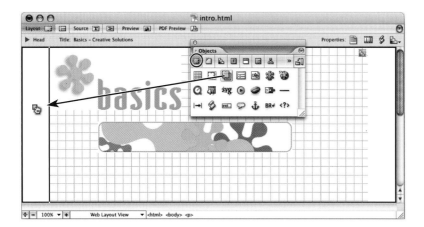

3   From the Basic set of the Objects palette, drag an Image object into the 100 x 100 pixel rectangle hanging off the frame anchor at the top of the page.

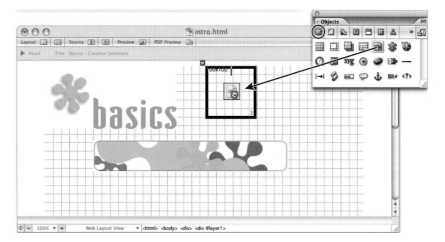

4   Drag from the Pick Whip button next to (Empty Reference!) in the Inspector palette to the file flower.gif in the images folder in the Files tab of the site window. Release the pointer when the filename is highlighted.

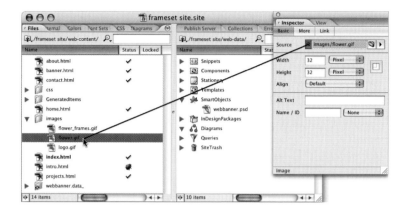

5   Select Layer 1 by clicking the yellow anchor at the top of the page. In the Inspector palette, enter **1** as Z-Index for this layer, in order for the content of this layer to appear on top of the other images on the page. Think of the Z-Index as a coordinate along the z-axis of a 3-dimensional coordinate system, with the z-axis coming out of the page plane towards you. Objects in a layer with a higher Z-Index appear above objects in layers with lower Z-Indices. You can also use a negative number as Z-Index to have objects appear behind other objects on the page.

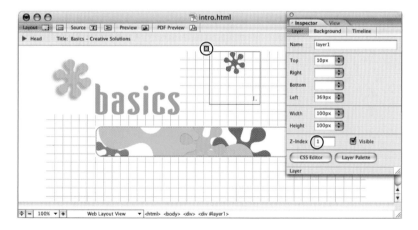

You can now reposition the layer box containing the image object anywhere on the page.

6   To select the layers bounding box, move the pointer towards the border line of the frame until the pointer changes to the hand icon, and then click the border line. *(See illustration on next page.)*

You will see handles appear at the corners, and at the center of the sides of the rectangle.

7   Click the border line (not the handles) of the selected layer's bounding box, and drag the rectangle to a position further down on the page, so that the image in the layer floats above the image of the larger animation.

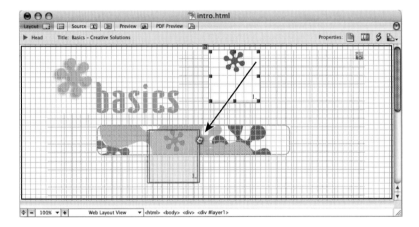

8   Choose File > Preview In > Default Browser, and wait for the page to get loaded in your browser. Note that the image in the layer is visible above the animation. Also note that if you resize the browser window width, the position of the image in the layer stays constant in respect to the top left corner of the window, not the top left corner of the layout grid, which always gets recentered when the page width changes. If you need to control the position of objects in layers relative to objects placed on a layout grid, the layout grid needs to be left aligned on the page.

Layers are useful if you have images that you want to overlap on a page (without layers you can't position images on a page so that the bounding boxes overlap). Furthermore, you can use GoLive's Timeline Editor to alter the position of the layer over time to create an animation effect.

Animate layers with the Timeline Editor

DHTML (or Dynamic HTML) has been around since the end of last century! Internet Explorer and Netscape Navigator (remember that?) have supported DHTML since version 4, way back in 1997 or 1998. Today it is everywhere, and you have no worries about compatibility issues when adding DHTML to your Web page.

1 Open the DHTML Timeline Editor by clicking the DHTML Timeline Editor button in the upper right corner of the intro.html document window.

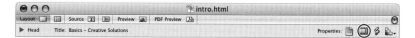

The DHTML Timeline Editor window will open with one track for each layer on the page. The track with the number 1 on the left corresponds to layer number 1. You can have multiple layers on a page, and animate them all simultaneously in the Timeline Editor. In this exercise however, you will work with only one layer.

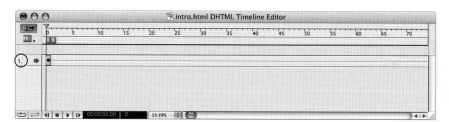

You animate a layer by inserting key frames at certain points along the track, and altering the frame's attributes at each key frame. You can change the frame's position, its stacking order or its visibility. The Web browser will interpolate the attributes between key frames. You can also specify how many frames per second (FPS) the Web browser should try to display. The higher the FPS rate, the smoother the animation, at least in theory. The speed of the computer limits the load a browser can handle. Start with the default of 15 FPS and see whether that works for your animation. In many cases, a lower FPS setting works just as well, while ensuring that the animation plays the same way on both slow and fast computers.

In the following steps, you will animate layer number 1 so that the flower image enters the page from the center left, moves down and right, halfway into the page, and then up and right, to exit the page near the top right corner.

2   Click the first (and for now, only) keyframe of track number 1 to select it. This will also select the layer with the flower.gif image in the intro.html document window.

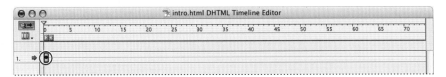

3   In the Layer pane of the Inspector palette, enter **100 px** (pixels) as position from Top and -**100 px** as position from Left. This will move the entire layer rectangle to the left and outside the page boundaries, making the flower.gif image invisible.

4   In the Timeline Editor window, create a new keyframe by Ctrl-clicking / Command-clicking track number 1 at approximately the 15-frame mark (you can reposition the keyframe later if necessary).

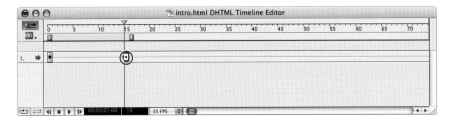

5   With the second keyframe selected, enter **250 px** (Top) and **250 px** (Left) in the Layer pane of the Inspector palette. The selected layer box with the flower.gif image will appear in the intro.html document window at that position. A gray line indicates the path that the top left corner of the layer box will take for the frames 1 through 15. *(See illustration on next page.)* At 15 FPS, it will take the image a second to move into the center of the page.

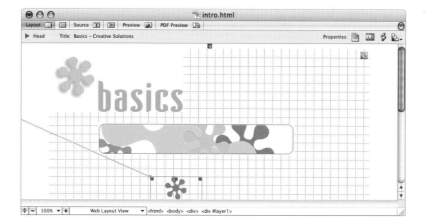

6   In the Timeline Editor window, create a third keyframe by Ctrl-clicking / Command-clicking track number 1 at approximately the 32-frame mark.

7   With the third keyframe selected, enter **-100 px** (Top) and **500 px** (Left) in the Layer pane of the Inspector palette. This will move the flower.gif image to the top and right, hiding it above the top edge of the page.

8   Select all three keyframes in the Timeline Editor window (Choose Edit > Select All or Shift-click each unselected keyframe). Then, in the Timeline pane of the Inspector palette, choose Curve from the Animation pop-up menu.

The path the image will take from keyframe to keyframe is now a smooth curve. As the last step, you will change the layer animation so that the flower.gif image will only enter the page shortly before the index.html page gets loaded.

9   With the three keyframes still selected in the Timeline Editor window, click the first keyframe, and drag it to the right to approximately the 70-frame mark (the two other keyframes will move to the right accordingly).

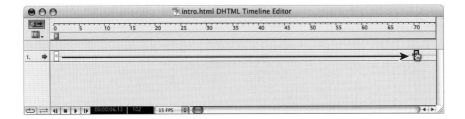

This will create a new, invisible keyframe at position zero, and only at frame 70 (not quite 5 seconds after the page has loaded), will the layer be set to visible, and the image start moving into the page. Shortly after the image moves out of the page, the index.html page should appear.

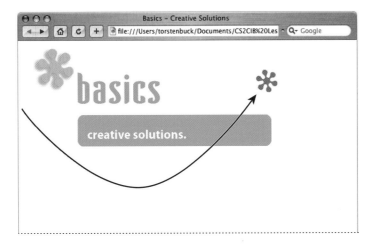

10 Preview your animation in your browser, make adjustments to the timing or positions of the image at the keyframes if necessary, and then save your work and relax. You're done!

Review

▶ **Review questions**

1 What is tweening?

2 How do you find broken links in GoLive?

3 What are actions in GoLive?

4 How can a page automatically load another page after a certain amount of time?

5 What can layers on a Web page be used for?

▶ **Review answers**

1 The Tween command in ImageReady automates the creation of additional frames in an animation. It does so by interpolating attributes of position, opacity and effect parameters, to generate a series of frames between two existing frames. In this way, ImageReady can significantly reduce the time required to create animation effects, such as having an object fade in (or out), or move across the scene.

2 If a page contains broken links, GoLive displays a bug icon next to the file name in the status column of the Files pane. In the document window, you can highlight elements causing a link error by choosing View > Show Link Warnings, or by clicking on the bug icon in the Main toolbar.

3 Actions in GoLive are scripts that are executed when triggered by specified events. An event can be something that the browser does (e.g. loading of a page), the user does (e.g. moving with the pointer over an image, or clicking something), or a point in time (e.g. in a timeline sequence). Actions can perform all sorts of things, from loading new images or pages, to opening alert or password windows, hiding and showing layers, or controlling the playback of sound or movies. GoLive provides a full set of pre-built actions ready for you to choose from (accessible via the Actions palette).

4 You can add a Refresh object to the head section of the page. You can specify the amount of time in seconds after which either the current page gets refreshed,

or a different page gets loaded. Refreshing is useful if your page displays live content pulled from a database that changes over time (e.g. a stock ticker or news headlines). You might load different pages to present a slide show, for example, where each page contains a Refresh object to load the next page in sequence.

5 The content of layers on a Web page can be formatted and positioned independently of each other. This way you can have images overlap on a page, for example. You can show and hide layers triggered by actions (e.g. to display a drop-down menu when moving over a menu button). Using the Timeline Editor, you can animate layers (e.g. change the layer's position on the page over time).

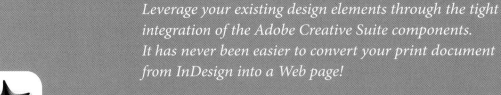

Leverage your existing design elements through the tight integration of the Adobe Creative Suite components. It has never been easier to convert your print document from InDesign into a Web page!

7 | Moving from Print to Web

Lesson overview

In this lesson, you'll learn how to do the following:

- Update Smart Objects in GoLive.

- Package for GoLive in InDesign.

- Import InDesign's Packages into GoLive.

- Use the CSS Editor.

This lesson will take about two hours to complete.

In Lesson 1, you set up a folder called CS2CIB Lessons on your hard disk. For this lesson, copy the Lesson07 folder from the *Adobe Creative Suite 2 Classroom in a Book* CD into the CS2CIB Lessons folder.

Editing source files of Smart Objects

InDesign's Package for GoLive feature is a wonderful help for easily repurposing print assets for use on the Web. In this lesson, you will add the content from the Newsletter designed in Lesson 4 to the Web site created in Lessons 5 and 6. If you haven't worked through those lessons yet, don't worry; the necessary files to work with are provided in the Lesson07 folder.

To start off, you will add a new navigation button to the Web banner, to make the newsletter section of the site accessible from the main page.

 1 Start Adobe GoLive, and open the file called frameset site.site inside the frameset site folder in the Lesson07 folder.

Notice that a few things have been added to the Web site created in Lessons 5 and 6. In the Files panel of the site window is a new folder called newsletter, containing several HTML pages and images. In the

SmartObjects folder of the Extras tab, a Photoshop file called nl-banner.psd has been included.

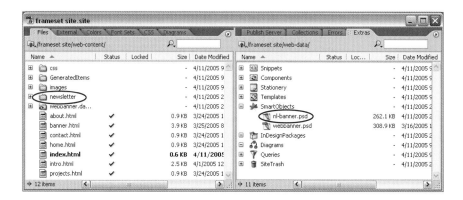

The newsletter folder contains the pages that will receive the content from the InDesign newsletter document created in Lesson 4. The nl-banner.psd Photoshop file is a navigation bar, used for the newsletter subsection of the Web site. This navigation bar was created in a manner similar to the creation of the Web banner / navigation bar on the main page in Lesson 5.

The first step is to open the Web banner / navigation bar from the main page, and add a navigation button that will link to the newsletter subsection.

2   In the Extras tab of the site window, select the file webbanner.psd (not the nl-banner.psd file!) inside the Smart Objects folder, and then choose Edit > Edit Original.

The file will open in Photoshop, the default editor for PSD files. Since it is ImageReady and not Photoshop that you will use to add the newsletter navigation button, all you need to do in Photoshop is to hand this file off to ImageReady.

3   In Photoshop, click the Edit in ImageReady button at the bottom of the toolbox.

Adding a new button to the navigation bar

The file will be opened in ImageReady. You need to add a button to the right of the existing buttons. To set the newsletter section apart from the other sections of the Web site, place the button flush right with the end of the creative solutions text in the upper part of the image. The color of the button will be Basics purple, with an RGB value of 191, 131, 185.

1   In the Color palette, select RGB sliders from the palette menu. Then enter RGB values of **191**, **131**, and **185** to set the foreground color to Basics purple.

2   In the toolbox, select the Tab Rectangle tool. Then, in the Options palette, select Create new shape layer, deselect Fixed Size, and set the Corner Radius to **10 px** (pixels).

A. Create New Shape Layer. B. No Fixed Size.

3   Position the pointer at the horizontal guide, 140 pixels from the top, and about 450 pixels from the left. Choose Ctrl-R (Windows) or Command-R (Mac OS) to turn on the Rulers if they are not visible already. Then, click and drag to a position 560 pixels from the left and to the bottom edge of the image. Release the pointer when ImageReady displays a guide indicating that the right edge of the rectangle is flush with the end of the text "creative solutions." (*See illustration on next page.*)

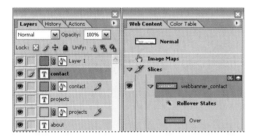

In the Layers palette, notice that a new layer has been added to the document. (Should the new layer not already be located at the top of the list in the Layers palette, click the layer and drag it to the topmost position in the list.)

4   In the Web Content palette, select the Normal state for the webbanner_contact slice. Then, in the Layers palette, select the contact text layer, just underneath the newly created layer. (If the Over state was selected in the Web Content palette, the contact text layer would have the color overlay layer effect applied, and you don't want to copy that in the next step.)

5   In the Layers palette, select Duplicate Layer from the palette menu. Click the resulting contact copy text layer, and drag it to the top of the list, above the shape layer containing the Basics purple rounded rectangle.

6 With the contact copy layer still selected in the Layers palette, select the Move tool in the toolbox, and then use the right arrow key repeatedly to move the text object (use the arrow key in combination with the Shift key for bigger jumps) until the copy of the contact text becomes visible over the purple rounded rectangle in the document window.

7 Select the Type tool in the toolbox. Double-click the word contact above the purple rounded rectangle to select it. Type **newsletter**, then select the Move tool, and use the left and right arrow keys to recenter the word in the button shape.

Adding a rollover state to the button

1 Select the shape layer containing the purple rounded rectangle in the Layers palette. Then, choose Layer Options in the palette menu.

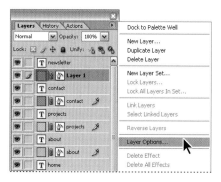

2 In the Layer Options dialog box, rename the layer to **newsletter** and click OK.

3 With the newsletter shape layer still selected in the Layers palette, choose Create Layer-Based Rollover from the Web Content palette menu. (*See illustration on next page.*)

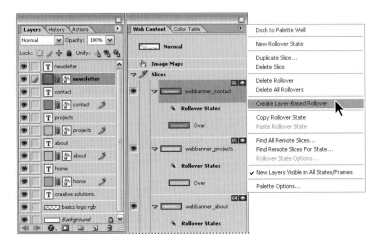

4   With the Over state of slice number 8 (the newsletter button slice) selected in the Web Content palette, select the newsletter text layer in the Layers palette. Then, choose Layer > Layer Style > Color Overlay. (If you have worked through Lesson 5, this might sound familiar.)

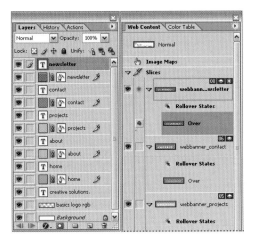

5   In the Color Overlay panel of the Layer Style dialog box, click the colored rectangle next to the Color Blend Mode pop-up menu to bring up the Color Picker dialog box. Enter the RGB values R: **191**, G: **131**, B: **185**, and then click OK to close the Color Picker dialog box.

6   Back in the Layer Style dialog box, set the Opacity of the Color Overlay to **50**%, and then click OK to close the dialog box.

7 In the Web Content palette, click alternately on the Normal and Over states of the newsletter button (slice number 8), and notice how the appearance of the button changes in the document window. In the Layers palette, observe the newsletter text layer has a layer style (the color overlay) applied that in the Over state, but not in the Normal state.

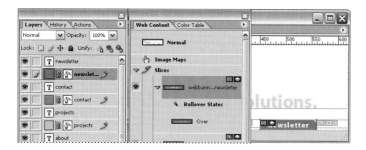

8 Choose File > Save, and then return to GoLive.

Updating modified Smart Objects in GoLive

Back in GoLive, you should notice that the modification date of the webbanner.psd file (in the SmartObjects folder in the Extra tab of the site window) now shows the time when the file was saved from within ImageReady. However, files derived from that Photoshop file (e.g. the Smart Object's webbanner.data folder in the Files tab), are not yet updated. You can explicitly trigger an update of site files that depend on files modified outside of GoLive by choosing Site > Update > Files Depending on Site Extras, or by selecting any modified files in the Extras tab, and choosing Site > Update > Files Depending on Selection. Alternatively, as shown here, you can watch those files being automatically updated the first time you open a document containing the Smart Object.

1   In the Files tab of the site window, double-click the banner.html file to open it.

GoLive automatically regenerates the content of the Smart Object on that page, reflecting the changes made to the webbanner.psd file.

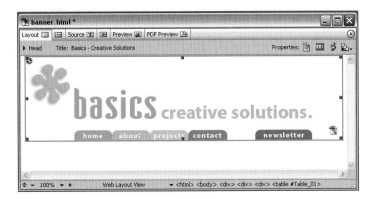

Better yet, the Alt Text and Links that were added earlier on to the Smart Object in GoLive are still there.

2   Select the Object Selection tool in the toolbox, and then click the home button to select it. Note that the entries in the Inspector palette are unaltered by the update to the webbanner.psd file from within ImageReady.

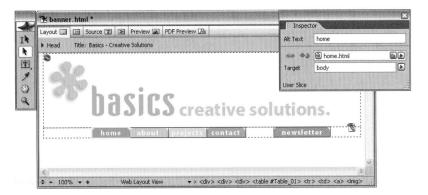

3   Select the newsletter button, and note that the entries in the Inspector palette for this new button are yet to be defined. Enter **newsletter** as Alt Text for this button.

4   In the Inspector palette, drag from the Pick Whip button, next to the broken chain icon, to the folder called newsletter in the Files tab in the site window. Don't release the pointer yet!

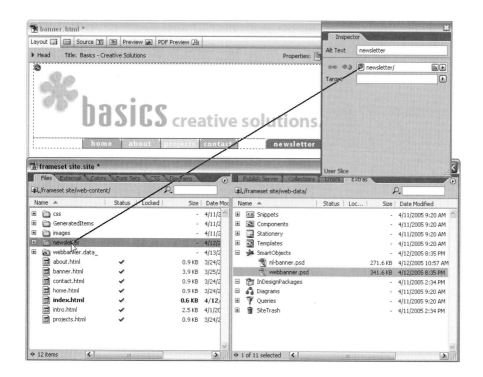

When you hold the pointer over the folder name for an instant, GoLive will open that folder in the Files tab, and display its content. The path of the currently displayed folder is shown at the top of the Files tab. (Move the pointer outside the file list if you want to display the content of the web-content folder again.)

5 Release the pointer when the file named index.html inside the newsletter folder in the Files tab is highlighted. The entry next to the Pick Whip button in the Inspector palette should now read newsletter/index.html.

6   In the Inspector palette, type **body** as Target for this link. (If this step is unclear, review in Lesson 5 about using frame sets and specifying target frames.)

7   Save the changes made to the banner.html page, and close its document window.

8   In the Files tab of the site window, double-click index.html (the one in the web-content folder, not the one in the web-content/newsletter subfolder) to open it.

9   In the index.html document window, select the Preview tab. Hold the pointer over the newsletter button to see its Over state (the color overlay applied to the text), and then click the newsletter button to see the content of the newsletter/index.html file appear in the lower part of the window (the body frame of the index.html page).

The index.html page inside the web-content/newsletter subfolder uses frame sets (as does the main index.html page). On the left, note a sub-navigation bar (corresponding to the different sections of the newsletter). Holding the pointer over the buttons will display their over states (the same color overlay effect as used for the main navigation bar). Clicking a button will load the corresponding page at the right (each page has a different colored half-circle on the left to match its navigation button). In the newsletter subfolder, in the Files tab of the site window, you will find one HTML file each for each sub-category, namely nl_news.html, nl_events.html, nl_program.html, nl_opinions.html, and nl_calendar.html. These files only contain the images necessary to visually indicate which button is currently selected in the navigation bar (a purple line across the top, connecting to the newsletter button) and in the sub-navigation bar (a colored half-circle on the left, connecting the respective buttons on the left). In the following steps, content will be added to the nl_news.html page, repurposing the assets used for creating the InDesign newsletter document in Lesson 4.

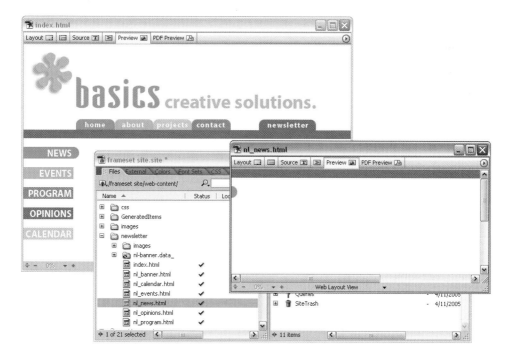

Preparing to use Package for GoLive in InDesign

1   Switch to InDesign, and open the file mynewsletterfinal.indd in the newsletter folder, inside the Lesson07 folder.

This is the final version of the newsletter created in Lesson 4. The masthead at the top of the page is a placed Illustrator file, and the photo of the red huts on the right hand side is a placed Photoshop file. In the following, those assets (the headline and main story on page 1, plus the picture which goes with it) will be repurposed for the design of the news page in the Web site. (*See illustration on next page.*)

The Package for GoLive command makes it extremely easy to reuse the content of an InDesign document for the creation of Web pages in GoLive. In the simplest case, the document can be exported from InDesign. GoLive will almost fully automatically create complete HTML pages very closely resembling the pages in the InDesign document.

Here in this lesson, you will pick and choose which elements from the InDesign document should be placed on the Web page. For this, you need to modify the layout to better integrate with the Web site design. For example, there is no need to reuse the newsletter masthead, but content in a tab needs to be placed under the Web banner already present in the Web site. Also, a specially designed navigation bar for the Web page, complete with rollover buttons, and links to other pages on the site, will fulfill the function of the table of contents in the InDesign document (the text on the colored background in the left column).

To preserve the appearance of text as closely as possible when going from print to Web, there are a few things to consider up-front. The text styling capabilities of InDesign far outshine what can be represented with even the latest HTML standards. Compromises have to be made. But, if you know what to look out for, good results can be achieved nonetheless.

First of all, the text to be reused on the Web page should be formatted using paragraph and character styles. The text formatting information can then be approximated by using Cascading Style Sheets (CSS) in GoLive. Text formatting not using paragraph and character styles will be lost when the package is opened in GoLive.

2   With the Type tool selected in the toolbox, click anywhere in the Vanishing Points! headline. Open the Paragraph Styles palette (Window > Type & Tables > Paragraph Styles), and confirm that this headline has been formatted using the Headline Paragraph Style.

3   Place the text cursor anywhere in the first paragraph of the main story (or select a portion of the paragraph's text), and confirm that this paragraph has been formatted using the Body Paragraph Style.

With this particular document, all text in the main story is formatted using the Body Paragraph Style. In general, it is advisable to go through the story one paragraph at a time, and check the formatting.

The next point to consider is the amount of text in a single story. While it is OK in a printed document to have text span several columns (and even be continued on another page), one should not have too much text in a single page in GoLive. The Package for GoLive command treats each text story as an entity. Drag this entity onto the page in GoLive and you'll end up with all the text of one story in a single text frame. To break a long story into more manageable chunks, it is better to either create additional text frames (without linking them!), and copy and paste sections of the story into each frame, or, more elegantly, and as shown later on, use GoLive's new smart text components when placing the story on the Web page. These smart Web components let you crop the text to display only part of the story in one text frame. Then another smart text component can be added to display another section of the story, for example on a second Web page, with a link to it from the first page.

That's about all there is to pay attention to at the moment; other issues will be covered while you are performing the Package for GoLive command.

Performing the Package for GoLive command

1   Choose File > Package for GoLive. If the button in the lower left corner of the Package Publication for GoLive dialog box reads Use Adobe Dialog, then click it. If it reads Use OS Dialog, you have the Adobe version of the dialog box selected, which is needed for the following step.

InDesign saves all the files of a Package for GoLive in a folder that you can specify in the Package Publication for GoLive dialog box. When importing such a package into GoLive, it is recommended that you add the files of the package to the GoLive site; i.e. by placing a copy of the entire Package for GoLive folder in the site's web-data/InDesignPackages folder. To avoid having two copies of the same data on your hard disk, export from InDesign directly into the web-data/InDesignPackages folder, or the GoLive site.

2   In the Package Publication for GoLive dialog box, navigate to the Lesson07 folder. Open the InDesignPackages folder, inside the frameset site/web-data folder, and then click Save.

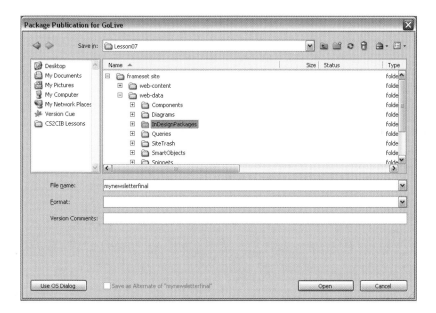

In the Publication for GoLive dialog box, one can specify whether to export all pages, or just a range of pages, or even just the selected elements (full page previews will be displayed in any case).

3   In the Publication for GoLive dialog box, enter **1** in the Range field to export only the elements on the front page of the newsletter.

The Encoding needs to match the text encoding used for the Web pages in the GoLive site. You can set the default encoding used for new pages in GoLive in the Encodings panel of the Preferences dialog box. The encoding for a given page in GoLive can be confirmed or changed by inspecting the Encode head element.

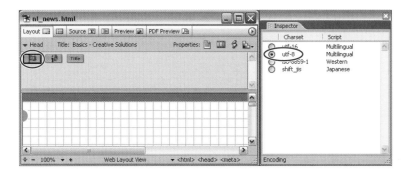

4   In the Package for GoLive dialog box, select UTF-8 (Unicode Transformation Format, which uses variable length sequences of 8-bit code units to encode characters) from the Encoding pop-up menu to match the encoding used for the pages in the GoLive site.

For files placed in the InDesign document, the original files can be included in the Package. This is useful because it enables GoLive to generate optimized images in sizes other than the original that still reference the original data. If you choose to include Formatted Images in the package, InDesign will create TIFF images with a resolution of 72 ppi, and the dimensions of the image in the InDesign document. If cropping is applied to a placed image, only the visible area of the image will be exported.

5   In the Package for GoLive dialog box, select to include Original Images, as well as Formatted Images, to allow for maximal flexibility when later importing elements from the package in GoLive.

6   Click Package, and wait for InDesign to complete the Package for GoLive command.

Opening the package in GoLive

1   Switch back to GoLive. Open the frameset site.site if it is not still open.

Had you exported the package from InDesign to a location outside the site's folder, you would now need to choose File > Import > From InDesign, and select the InDesign package file. GoLive would place a copy of the entire package folder (after asking for confirmation), in the web-data/InDesignPackages folder. But, since the package has already been sneaked into that folder through the back door, you'll need to explicitly tell GoLive that there's a new package in the folder that it should be aware of.

2 Right-click / Control-click the InDesignPackages folder name, in the Extras tab of the site window, then choose Update > Refresh Selection from the pop-up menu.

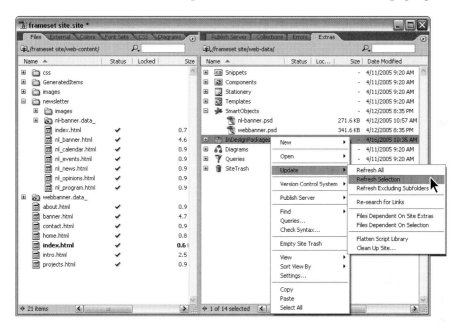

3 Click the plus sign to the left of the InDesignPackages folder name, and note the mynewsletterfinal package in the expanded view.

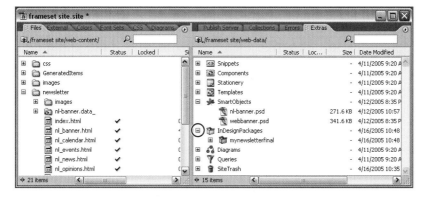

Note: Although the mynewsletterfinal package has a plus sign to the left of its name, this folder's view cannot be expanded.

4   Double-click the mynewsletterfinal package icon to open the package window. In the InDesign Layout tab, observe a thumbnail view of the first page of the InDesign newsletter. Since this package only contains one page of the InDesign document, the First, Previous, Next and Last Page buttons on the lower right corner of the package window are disabled. Otherwise, one could flip through the pages of the exported document to find the elements to be added to the Web site. You can also resize the package window, and zoom in and out as desired.

In the Assets tab, all available elements are in the package, listed by Stories (i.e. text blocks), and Images. Those elements could be dragged from here into the Web page document window or, as described below, from the more visual InDesign Layout tab.

By clicking the HTML Preview tab, you can have GoLive try to convert the entire page from the package to an HTML page equivalent. You have some control over the conversion process via a Layout Scaling slider in the Main toolbar. Then you'd choose Export as HTML page from the palette menu, to create an entire HTML page, preserving as much of the original page layout as possible, and creating a page that is ready to be added to the Web site. But as mentioned earlier, for this lesson you will pick and choose which elements to incorporate into the design of the Web page, and therefore not use this option.

5   Select the InDesign Layout tab in the mynewsletterfinal package window. You will drag the elements from here. In the site window, double-click the nl_news.html page icon (inside the newsletter folder in the Files tab), to open it in its document window. It is to here that you will drag the elements.

6 In the InDesign Layout tab of the mynewsletterfinal package window, hold the pointer over the page.

GoLive will highlight the various elements available for dragging onto the HTML page. Also displayed will be additional information for each highlighted element, like the type and name of the asset. To highlight the Photoshop image, the pointer needs to be moved over the picture, but between the columns of the main story text; this is one situation where identifying and dragging an element from the Assets tab might be easier.

7 Click the Vanishing Points! headline text item to select it, and then open the Inspector palette to define the Asset Conversion Settings for this story element.

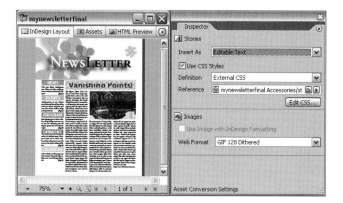

Text of a story can be inserted as Editable Text, Smart Component, or Snapshot Image.

You can use Snapshot Image to preserve text styling that normally would not be represented on Web pages using CSS text formatting. Examples are swash characters and ligatures, or the use of a specific font. Snapshot Image would represent the text appearance as an image, but the text content would get lost (i.e. the text in the image cannot be selected or copied and pasted or searched). Obviously, you only want to use this option in rare circumstances. In such cases it's a good idea to also enter the original text as Alt Text for the image on the page.

Text added as a Smart Component to the page keeps a link to the original text in the InDesign document. If the text gets edited in InDesign, and then repackaged, the Smart Component in GoLive also gets updated to reflect the changes. Furthermore, the text can be cropped to only display part of the original story on a Web page. But the text can't be edited directly in the GoLive Web page document.

Editable Text converts the text to regular text on the Web page, and this text can then be edited directly in GoLive if necessary. GoLive does not keep a link to the original text in the InDesign document, so changes made there will not automatically be reflected on the Web page.

For the Vanishing Points! headline, the Editable Text option seems to be the most practical.

8   Select Editable Text from the Insert As pop-up menu in the Inspector palette.

The use of Cascading Style Sheets (CSS) can help maintain consistent text formatting throughout a Web site. This also allows for quick updates to the appearance of text in all pages—be it one, ten, or hundreds of pages—referring to a common CSS. Think of CSS as the equivalent to paragraph and character styles in an InDesign document.

The Inspector palette offers the choice of using an Internal CSS, External CSS, or none. An Internal CSS applies to only the text within the current HTML page; an External CSS is stored separately (externally) and can be shared by many HTML pages. This is what will be used for this project. When the text element in the package window was selected, GoLive added an external style sheet, called styles.css, to the site. That sheet is located in the web-content/mynewsletterfinal Accessories/styles folder, visible in the Files tab of the site window.

9   With the headline still selected in the package window, make sure Use CSS Styles is selected in the Inspector palette. If necessary, select External CSS from the Definition pop-up menu, and choose Set Reference to Package CSS from the menu to the right of the Reference field.

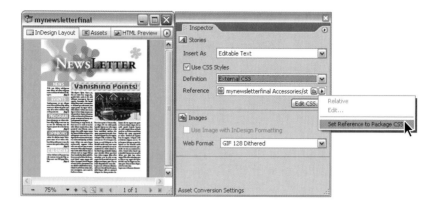

10 With all text conversion options specified in the Inspector palette, drag the headline element from the package window onto the nl_news.html document window near the top left corner of the page.

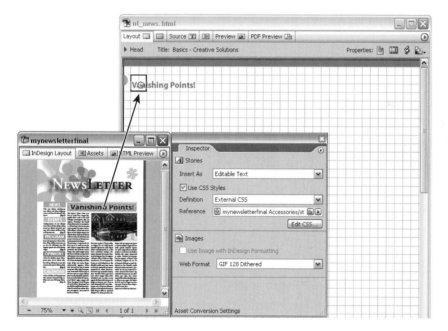

11 Select the placed object on the page (the eight handles of the bounding box should be visible). *(See illustration on next page.)*

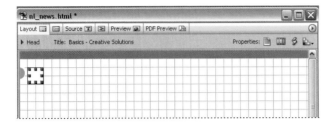

12 Grab the lower right handle, and try to resize the bounding box; it will snap to a size large enough to hold the placed headline in the selected text style.

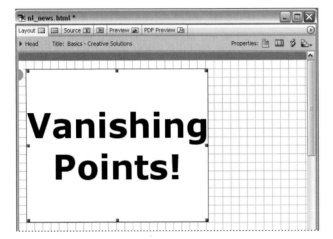

Obviously, the way this headline is formatted is much too large for this Web page. You will now edit the external style sheet that governs the formatting of the headline, to adjust the design for the Web page.

Using the CSS Editor

From the paragraph styles in the InDesign package content, GoLive derived so-called CSS class styles. Class styles can be applied to a text selection on a HTML page, and allow control over a wide array of formatting options, like text color, typeface and point size, and alignment and margins. GoLive's built-in CSS Editor can be used to customize these settings.

1 In the toolbox, select the Standard Editing tool, then click anywhere inside the headline text. A blinking insertion cursor will appear, but don't enter any text now!

2   Open the CSS palette (Window > CSS) to see that for the current paragraph (the head*line* is in fact a paragraph, at least from a text layout point of view), a class style named ParHeadline has already been applied.

3   The definition for the ParHeadline class style is stored in the external style sheet called styles.css, located in the web-content/mynewsletterfinal Accessories/styles folder. To edit this definition, choose Edit in "styles.css" from the pop-up menu next to the class style's name.

The CSS Editor window will open, with the ParHeadline class style selected for editing.

Note: Class style names are preceded by a point (.) in the CSS Definitions list (e.g. .ParHeadline). This is to differentiate them from Element Styles (myelementstyle), ID Styles (#myidstyle), or styles applied to standard HTML formatting tags (body, p, h1, h2, ...).

4   Select the Selector and Properties panel on the right side of the CSS Editor window.

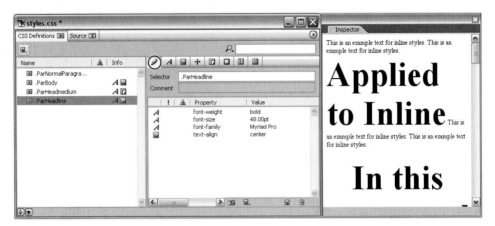

The font formatting properties for weight, size, and family, as well as text alignment, have been directly derived from the settings in the InDesign document. The Inspector palette gives a preview of how this style looks by applying it to sample text. The typographers amongst you might notice that in the picture above the preview window, the font displayed is not actually Myriad Pro. Rather, it's the default font (in this case Times New Roman), in its bold weight and a point size of 48 point. A Web browser uses this default font if Myriad Pro is not installed on the system. To increase the chances of getting a result that better matches your design intention, a whole list of typefaces can be specified for each class style. A Web browser can pick a font from that list (if the font is installed on the system), before having to resort to the default typeface.

5   Select the Font Properties panel on the right side of the CSS Editor window, and then select Myriad Pro in the list of fonts (there's only this one font in the list). Then, click the Create new font pop-up menu in the lower right corner of the window (to the left of the Delete icon).

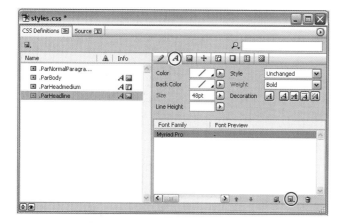

6   From the list of typefaces in the pop-up menu, select a typeface that more closely resembles Myriad Pro than does Times New Roman. Possible candidates (that are also likely to be on the computers that will be used to view your Web site) are Arial, Helvetica, or Verdana. You might find Myriad or Myriad Web in the All Fonts sub-menu. These are, of course, excellent replacement candidates for Myriad Pro. Add them all, one after the other, to the list of fonts in the Font Properties panel. (To add a font that is not installed on your system, the source code of the CSS can be edited manually.)

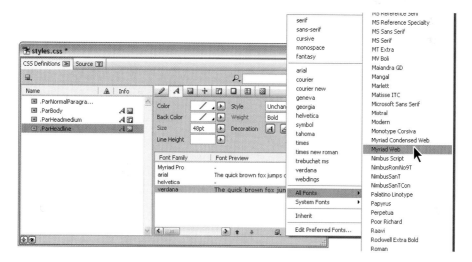

7   A Web browser will try to find a matching font in the order listed. To move the entry for Myriad Web higher up, select its name in the list, and then click the Move item upwards icon repeatedly. *(See illustration on next page.)*

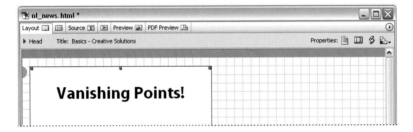

8   Enter **24 pt** as Size for the font (instead of the currently too big 48 pt).

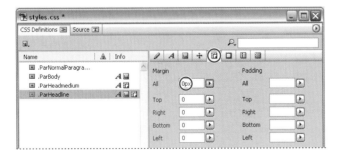

In the nl_news.html document window, the font size now looks okay, but there is still some unwanted top margin visible in the text in the frame. This can also be adjusted in the CSS Editor.

9   Select the Margin and Padding Properties panel, on the right side of the CSS Editor window. Enter **0 px** as value for All (this will automatically assign the value 0 as Top, Right, Bottom, and Left margin).

10 In the nl_news.html document window, resize the text frame to a width of **288** pixels and a height of **48** pixels. Use the Main toolbar to position and resize the frame by entering numeric values in appropriate fields. Position its top left corner at **16** pixels from the left and **32** pixels from the top of the page.

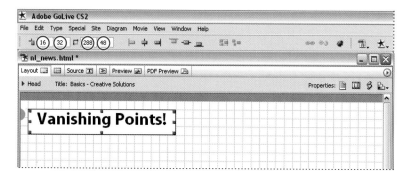

You've now created a formatting template for all headlines that will be added from the InDesign package to the Web page (although in this example there is only this one headline). As long as the Web pages are linked to the same external cascading style sheet document, you will have established a consistent look throughout the site.

11 Save the styles.css file in the CSS Editor window, the nl_news.html document window, and the site window. Use the Preview tab in the document window of the main index.html to see how the content of the nl_news.html page would look in its final context. At this point, you may close the CSS Editor window of the styles.css file.

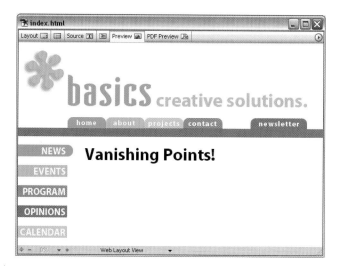

Inserting stories as Smart Text Components

1   In the package window, click the first column of the main story to select it. Then, choose Insert As Smart Component, for the Story text in the Inspector palette. Use the same external style sheet that was used for the headline text.

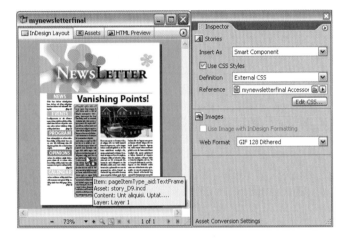

2   From the package window, drag the first column of the main story onto the nl_news.html document page. Release the pointer when the rectangle is positioned exactly under the headline text frame, with the top left corner 16 pixels from the left (the width of one box of the background grid), and 80 pixels (five boxes) from the top of the page.

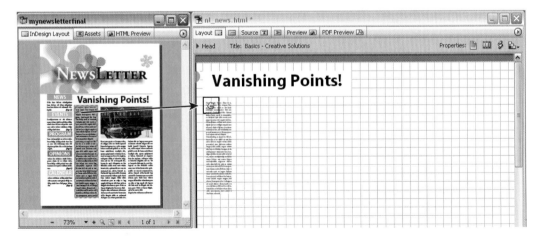

Even though only the first text column was highlighted when dragging from the package window, the text of the entire story will be placed in this Smart Component.

3   In the nl_news.html document window, drag the width of this Smart Component text frame out to 288 pixels. Release the pointer when GoLive draws a line at the right, indicating that the text box is flush with the text box of the headline.

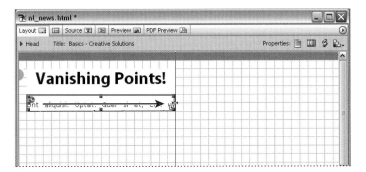

4   Select the layout grid in the nl_news.html page and set the height to 900 in the Inspector palette. Then select the text frame again (move the pointer over the text frame edges until you see the hand icon, then click to select the frame and have the position and dimensions displayed in the Main toolbar) and set the height to 800 pixels in the Main toolbar.

Scrolling down in the nl_news.html document window will show you that even this extremely long text frame is not long enough to hold the text of the entire story. You will have to resort to displaying only part of the story in this frame, and the rest in a different text frame. You could either add a new page to the site for this additional text frame (with a link to jump to it), or try to fit the text under the picture that will later be placed in the top right corner of the page. But first, you will use Smart Component's crop feature to specify the amount of text to be displayed in the current frame.

5   In the nl_news.html document window, click anywhere inside the text frame of the main story. You will not be able to place an insertion pointer (Smart Components are not editable directly in GoLive), but the Inspector palette will offer a Crop Text button. *(See illustration on next page.)*

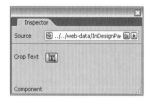

6   In the Inspector palette, click the Crop Text button. The Main toolbar will enable you to specify how to crop the text.

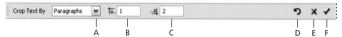

*A. Crop by Characters, Words, Paragraphs, or Custom Breaks. **B.** Enter start of selection. **C.** Enter end of selection. **D.** Remove any existing cropping information. **E.** Cancel and exit the crop mode. **F.** Accept the currently specified cropping, and exit the crop mode.*

7   A good way to crop the story text is by Paragraphs. Select Paragraphs from the Crop Text pop-up menu in the Main toolbar. Enter **1** as start and **2** as end of selection (i.e. crop from first to second paragraph inclusively). Click the check mark icon in the Main toolbar to accept the cropping, and to exit the crop mode.

If the remaining text of the story should appear in another text frame, a second Smart Component could be created from the same story in the package window, with the text cropped from the third to the last paragraph.

If the story text later gets edited in InDesign, and repackaged for GoLive, Smart Components that are dependent on the package will get updated in GoLive, preserving the customized cropping (and style sheet) settings.

Placing images from a package

As a last step, you will place the photo of the red huts on the Web page. The image can be placed using the same dimensions as in the original InDesign document, or resized to better fit the design of the Web page. The image compression settings can be specified as well.

1   In the package window, hold the pointer over the picture of the red huts.

You will notice that it is difficult to highlight or select the image, because GoLive highlights the second or third text column of the main story instead. That is because the image was placed on top of the text columns in InDesign. The image only gets highlighted if you hold your pointer between the two existing columns. For cases like this, where it is difficult to select a particular object on the page because it is overlapping with another object, you can use the Assets tab in the package window to select the object.

2   Click the Assets tab in the package window. Click the plus sign next to Images to see a list of all images in the package.

If the image can be made out by its name, you could now select it from the list. But especially for pictures, it is probably easier to select from a list of image thumbnails.

3   With the Assets tab selected in the package window, click the Thumbnail view icon in the lower left corner of the window. Hold the pointer over the story assets to see the beginning of its text content displayed in a floating text box. Scroll down to see thumbnail images of the two pictures in the package.

A. *Details view.* B. *Thumbnail view.*

4   Click the thumbnail image of the picture with the red huts to select it. In the Inspector palette, deselect Use Image with InDesign Formatting, because the image

will need to be resized to fit in the narrow column to the right of the story on the Web page. Choose Open Save For Web Dialog from the Web Format pop-up menu. When the image is placed on the page, the image compression options and size can be set in a Save for Web dialog box that you might already be familiar with from Photoshop or ImageReady.

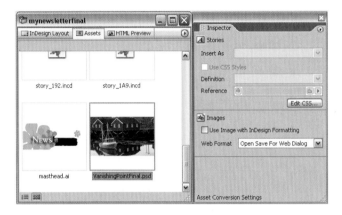

5   Right-click / Control-click the VanishingPointFinal.psd thumbnail image, and choose Reveal in InDesign Layout from the pop-up menu. The image will be highlighted in the InDesign Layout tab of the package window, ready to be dragged on the page.

6   Drag the VanishingPointFinal.psd thumbnail image from the package window onto the nl_news.html document window. Release the pointer when the little black rectangle is flush at the top with the headline text frame, and the width of one background grid to the right of it.

7 In the Save For Web dialog box, do the following: Select JPEG Medium from the Preset pop-up menu, click the Image Size tab and, with Constrain Proportions selected, enter a Width of **192** pixels. Click Apply, and then click Save.

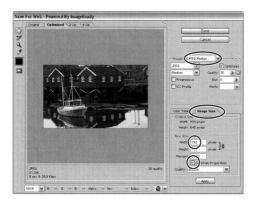

8 In the nl_news.html document window, click the lower right corner handle of the selected image frame, then drag to the right and down to enlarge the frame to fit the entire image.

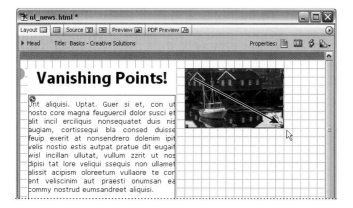

That's it! Drag another smart text component underneath the picture and fill it with more text from the main story if so desired. You're the designer and know best how to present your content. There is of course much more to discover about the improved integration of InDesign and GoLive via the Package for GoLive command than can be demonstrated in this one lesson. But by now you should feel familiar enough to continue discovering the many available options on your own.

Review

▶ **Review questions**

1 Why is it beneficial to design the Normal state of rollover buttons directly in ImageReady and not in Photoshop?

2 What command do you need to invoke in GoLive after extra files, such as the original Photoshop file of a Smart Object, have been modified outside of GoLive?

3 What is a quick way to convert a page (or pages) of a document created in InDesign into a Web page in GoLive?

4 Why is it a good idea to choose to include the original image files when exporting a Package for GoLive?

5 What does CSS stand for?

▶ **Review answers**

1 ImageReady has a tool called Tab Rectangle tool, specifically designed to create rollover buttons. ImageReady can use the shape layer created with that tool to define slices and rollover states for the buttons.

2 Choose Site > Update > Files Depending on Site Extras, or select the modified files in the Extras tab and choose Site > Update > Files Depending on Selection.

3 In InDesign, export the document as Package for GoLive. After importing the package into GoLive, select the HTML Preview tab in the package window, adjust the Layout Scaling in the Main toolbar, and then choose Export As HTML from the palette menu in the package window. This will generate ready-to-use HTML pages closely resembling the original layout in InDesign.

4 Enclosing original image files allows GoLive to create web optimized images directly from these files if necessary; e.g. if you want an image to have different dimensions on the Web page than in the InDesign document. In general, this will yield better results than re-sampling from an already resized image.

5 CSS stands for Cascading Style Sheets, which can help you to maintain consistent text formatting on your Web page, similar to paragraph and character styles in InDesign.

Guidelines for a Slide Presentation

- **Brevity**
  - Reduce excessive content to a short list of key messages.
- **Simplicity**
  - Tables should not be too complex as it is strenuous to concentrate.
  - Use animation and slide transition effects sparingly to not bore your audience or detract from your message.
- **Consistency**
  - Use the same typefaces throughout.
  - Position the titles and logos on the same place in each slide.
  - Consistency makes information easier to absorb.

How you convey your ideas is important. All it takes is Adobe InDesign, Adobe Acrobat, and a few simple rules to create a presentation that's painless, persuasive, and engaging.

8 Presenting with Style

Lesson overview

In this lesson, you'll learn how to do the following:

- Set up a document to create a slide presentation in Adobe InDesign.
- Edit the master page.
- Place artwork.
- Create paragraph and character styles.
- Add hyperlinks.
- Export as PDF, including hyperlinks and other interactive elements.
- Set initial view options in Adobe Acrobat.
- Present in full screen mode.
- Navigate a PDF document.

This lesson will take about an hour to complete.

In Lesson 1, you set up a folder called CS2CIB Lessons on your hard disk. For this lesson, copy the Lesson08 folder from the *Adobe Creative Suite 2 Classroom in a Book* CD into the CS2CIB Lessons folder.

Using InDesign for your presentation

Whether presenting a slideshow to a client or an audience, it is vitally important that your slides are convincing in both design and content.

Why presentation applications other than InDesign don't yet support good typography is a mystery. The most obvious shortcoming is the lack of kerning capabilities, which enable a user to create visually equal spaces between all letters, so that the eye can move smoothly along the text. Typeface designers usually spend a considerable amount of time preparing kerning tables, in which they predefine the optimal spacing between pairs of letters to improve the readability of a font. Although this information is included with the font files, some presentation programs continue to ignore the kerning tables. In the illustration below, the letter combinations Wo and Ty have been kerned in the second line, making their spacing visually consistent with the spacing between the other letters in the line.

Working with Type
Working with Type

InDesign not only kerns text properly, but also provides access to other advanced typographic features in OpenType fonts. Also, for working with graphics, you can rely on InDesign's effective integration with Photoshop and Illustrator.

If the resolution of the display device on which the slide show will be presented is known, it is easy to create a document configured with an exactly matching width and height in pixels. That way, no text or images will get scaled, which can cause distortions. When presenting to only one or two people, it is possible to present directly on a PowerBook screen, with its elegant horizontal format. In this case, you can set the presentation to 1152 x 768 pixels. If it's necessary to use a projector, that resolution won't normally be supported, so it is better to set up the document for 1024 x 768 pixels.

Note: When presenting slides in Acrobat in Windows (with a usual monitor resolution of 96 ppi), one can compensate for the higher screen resolution by choosing a custom resolution of 72 Pixels/Inch in the Page Display panel of the Preferences dialog box.

Setting up the document

The project starts by creating a master page for the slides.

1   Start InDesign. If greeted by the welcome screen, click Close.

2   Choose Edit > Preferences > Units & Increments (Windows) or InDesign > Preferences > Units & Increments (Mac OS), set the Horizontal and Vertical Ruler Units to Points, and then click OK to close the Preferences dialog box.

3 Choose File > New > Document. In the New Document dialog box, set the page size to **1024 pt** for Width and **768 pt** for Height. Select Landscape Orientation. Set Number of Pages to **20**, turn Facing Pages off, and then click OK.

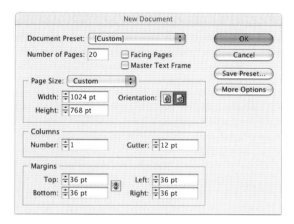

4 Save the document in the Lesson08 folder and name it **mypresentation.indd**.

Editing master pages

Elements that appear on every slide of the presentation, things like color bars and the company logo, should be designed and placed on the master page. The master page is also where you define text frames for the headline and the main text area.

1 To select the master page for editing, double-click the A-Master page icon in the Pages palette.

2 Using the Rectangle Frame tool, draw a graphic frame the height of the page and about 150 points wide.

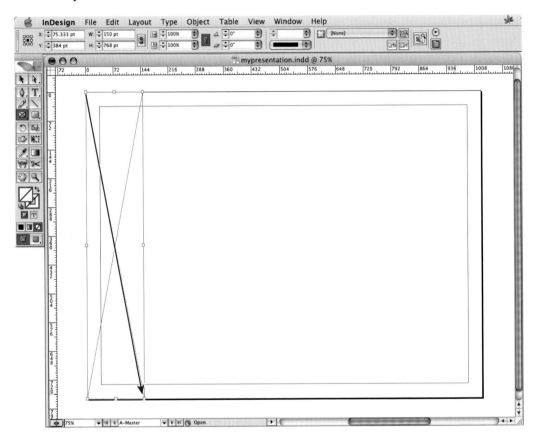

Note: Moving the pointer over the various tools in the toolbox will display the name of each tool, as well as the keyboard shortcut to select a particular tool.

3 With the frame still selected, place artwork by choosing File > Place and, in the Place dialog box, deselect Show Import Options and select Replace Selected Item, and then select the slidebanner.eps file in the Lesson08 folder, and click Open.

Now, a vertical colored banner on the left side of each slide is displayed.

4   To have the company logo appear on the lower right corner of each slide, create another frame, about 240 pt wide and 110 pt high, just inside the document margins at the lower right side.

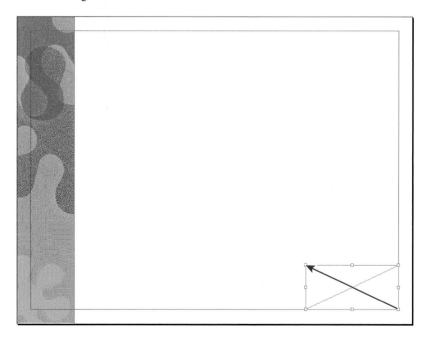

5   Place the file slidelogo.ai from the Lesson08 folder into that frame, the same way you placed the slidebanner.eps file in step 7. Note that the logo artwork is much larger than the frame it is loaded into.

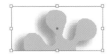

6   Choose Object > Fitting > Fit Content Proportionally to fit the image into the frame.

Setting up text frames

Now that the graphic appearance is set for the presentation, defining where the text will go is next. For this, default text frames must be prepared on the master page—one for the headers and one for the main text.

1   With the Type tool, draw a frame just inside the documents margins in the top right corner, as shown in the illustration. You will adjust the dimensions of the frame in the next step.

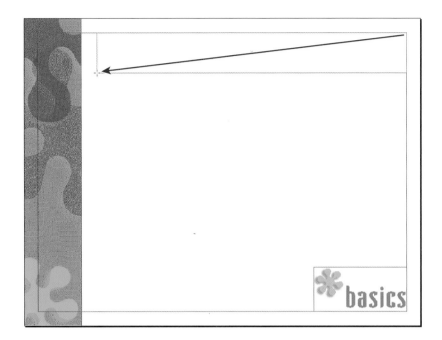

2   Select the frame with the Selection tool. In the Control palette, set the top right corner as reference point, and then enter **800 pt** as width and **100 pt** as height.

3   Alt-Shift-click / Option-Shift-click the frame, and drag the pointer to create a second frame underneath.

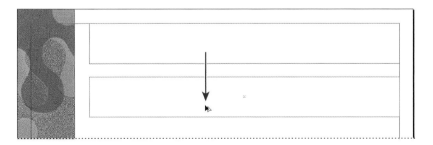

4   In the Control palette, with the reference point unchanged, enter **170 pt** as distance from top of page and **420 pt** as height for the frame.

Defining paragraph styles

The last thing to do on the master page is set up paragraph styles for the headline text, and for the default style of a bullet point list.

1   With the Type tool selected, click into the text frame for the headline. Type **Title**, which will act as dummy-copy, and then double-click the word to select it.

2   In the Control palette, choose the sans serif typeface, Myriad Pro Bold (which gets installed with your Creative Suite 2) in a size of **50 pt**.

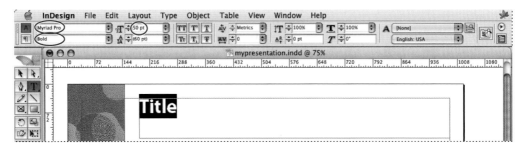

For slides, it is general practice to use a flush left paragraph style. The frame you created is high enough to allow for titles with up to 2 lines.

Now, your formatted text is used to create a paragraph style.

4   With the word Title (in the correct typeface and size) selected, choose New Paragraph Style from the Paragraph Styles palette menu. In the New Paragraph Style dialog box, give the new style a descriptive name like **Title Style** and click OK.

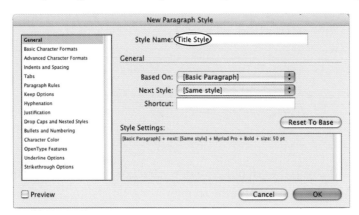

5   With the headline text still selected, apply that new paragraph style by clicking the Title Style entry in the Paragraph Styles palette

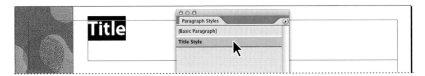

Starting paragraphs with bullets

That was easy. Setting up different levels in the main text frame is a bit trickier, but once it's done it's a snap to use.

1   With the Type tool selected, click in the main text frame and type **Bullet Level 1**. Again, this is only placeholder text, which will be overwritten in each slide.

2   Triple-click anywhere in this text to select the entire line. In the Control palette, again choose Myriad Pro Bold, but this time select a size of **36 pt**.

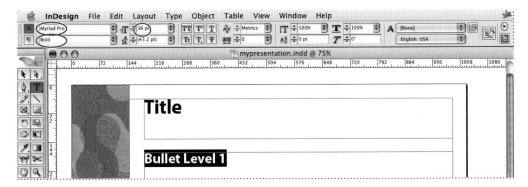

Note: Serif typefaces are good for readability in long texts, but for bullet lists—usually short, one-line sentences—a sans serif typeface often does a better job of getting the message across.

3   With the text still selected, choose New Paragraph Style from the Paragraph Styles palette menu. Call this style **Bullet Level 1**, but don't click OK yet. There are more formatting options that you can set to achieve quite sophisticated results.

4　To have each bullet item in your presentation start with a bullet point, select Bullets and Numbering from the list on the left in the New Paragraph Style dialog box. Then select Bullets from the List Type pop-up menu, and click OK to close the New Paragraph Style dialog box

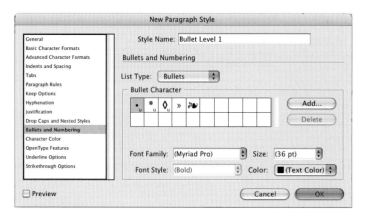

5　With the text still selected, apply that new paragraph style by clicking the Bullet Level 1 entry in the Paragraph Styles palette

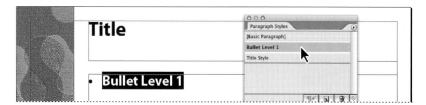

With the paragraph style defined the way it is now, text that is longer than one line would align on the left at the bullet point, as shown in the following illustration.

- **Lestio consequ ipsusci ex euis alit luptat.**
- **Ummy nulputatet, commodo core dipsum ea faccummy nos dolobor.**
- **Quam dipsuscidunt dit alit volore diam vendip-it lor se do exerostie velit alit lore vent lortismod dolor sim do diam dolortis esequat praeseniat.**
- **Enit la conse conse tin hendrer alit dolenim.**

As shown in the following illustration, text that's longer than one line looks better when any additional line is aligned with the beginning of the first word rather than with the bullet point.

- **Lestio consequ ipsusci ex euis alit luptat.**
- **Ummy nulputatet, commodo core dipsum ea faccummy nos dolobor.**
- **Quam dipsuscidunt dit alit volore diam vendipit lor se do exerostie velit alit lore vent lortismod dolor sim do diam dolortis esequat praeseniat.**
- **Enit la conse conse tin hendrer alit dolenim.**

To make this happen, you need to set up tab stops and format the paragraph to left align on the first tab stop, with the first line—that's the line with the bullet point—hanging out to the left.

Modifying paragraph styles

1 With the Bullet Level 1 text still selected in the main text frame, double-click the Bullet Level 1 entry in the Paragraph Styles palette to open the Paragraph Style Options dialog box. Select Tabs from the list on the left. Select the Left-Justified Tab button, and then click in the white area above the ruler at 36 pt from the left. If necessary, you can adjust the tab position by entering **36 pt** as X value.

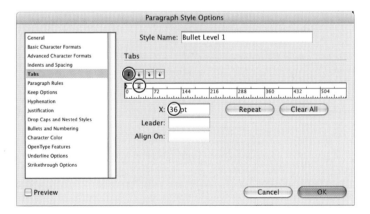

2 Now, select Indents and Spacing from the list on the left, set Left Indent to **36 pt** and First Line Indent to **-36 pt**. To add extra space at the end of each paragraph, enter **10 pt** as Space After. *(See illustration on next page.)* Click OK.

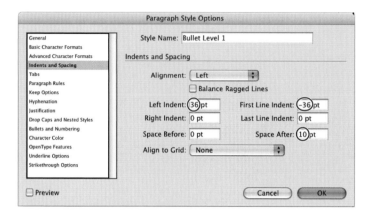

These steps modified an existing paragraph style. You can also create a new paragraph style based on an existing paragraph style, as shown here for a second level bullet text.

3   Position the cursor at the end of the Bullet Level 1 text and press Enter / Return, and then type **Bullet Level 2** (the bullet point at the begin of the line will appear automatically).

4   With the cursor still blinking at the end of line 2, select New Paragraph Style from the Paragraph Styles palette. Name this new style **Bullet Level 2**. Make sure that Bullet Level 1 is selected in the Based On pop-up menu.

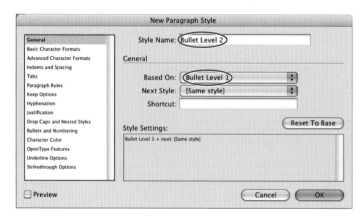

For the level 2 text we want a regular (not bold) typeface in a smaller size. These adjustments can be made in the Basic Character Formats panel.

5   Select Basic Character Formats from the list on the left, and then select Regular from the Font Style pop-up menu and enter **24 pt** as Size.

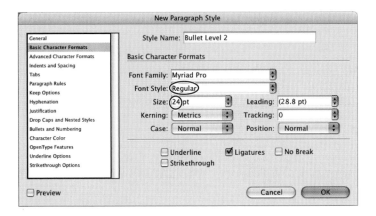

6   Select Indents and Spacing from the list on the left, and then set the left indent to
72 pt (2 times 36 pts) and leave the first line indent at -36 pt. Reduce Space After to **6 pt**.
Click OK to close the New Paragraph Style dialog box.

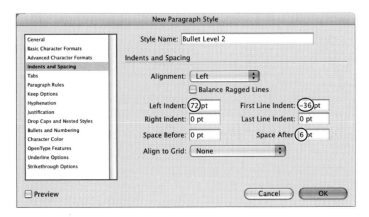

7   With the cursor still blinking at the end of line 2, click the newly defined Bullet
Level 2 entry in the Paragraphs Styles palette to see how the formatting is applied to
the bullet item text; the text is indented and the typeface size reduced. Using these
paragraph styles enables you to quickly change the hierarchy of information.

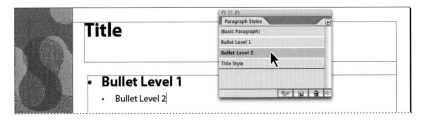

Adding interactive elements

With InDesign, a hyperlink can be created from either text or a graphic in the document to a hyperlink destination, which, in the simplest case, is just another page in the same document—much like the hyperlinks on Web pages. These hyperlinks can later be included when the document is exported as a PDF file. When viewed in Acrobat, clicking the hyperlink will let the reader jump to the page defined as a hyperlink destination.

The Basics logo in the lower right corner of the slide will be turned into a hyperlink, so that when the presenter clicks it, the presentation will jump to a specific page. For example page 2, which might contain the table of contents that needs to be referred to repeatedly throughout the presentation. Covering an area with a graphic frame, making the frame itself invisible, and then associating a hyperlink with that frame makes a clickable area.

1   Choose the Rectangle Frame tool and draw a rectangle around the Basics logo; the rectangle defines the clickable area.

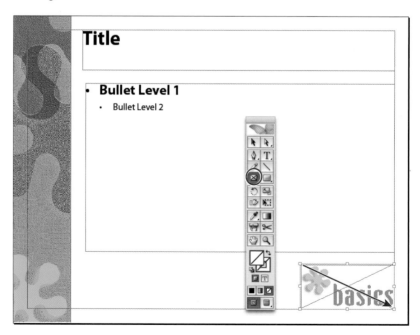

2   Open the Hyperlinks palette (Window > Interactive > Hyperlinks), and with the frame still selected, choose New Hyperlink from the Hyperlinks palette menu.

3 In the New Hyperlink dialog box, select Page from the Destination Type pop-up menu and select Page 2 as the page number of the Destination. You may want to give the hyperlink a distinctive name, although most of the time, hyperlinks will not be searched for by name. Instead, selecting a design element on a page will automatically highlight the corresponding hyperlink—if any—in the Hyperlinks palette. Don't forget to select Invisible Rectangle from the Appearance Type pop-up menu. Click OK.

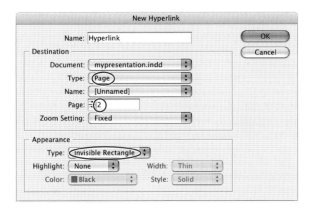

Note: *InDesign lets you insert sound, video, and other multimedia into what would otherwise be a static presentation. Placing a QuickTime movie in InDesign is as easy as placing a graphic. Exported to PDF, it can create a stunning multimedia presentation.*

Exporting hyperlinks and interactive elements

If at this point you're curious how the hyperlink will look and work when displayed in Acrobat, you can do a quick test cycle.

1 Choose File > Export, and select Adobe PDF as Format in the Export dialog box. Navigate to the Lesson08 folder, accept **mypresentation.pdf** as file name, and click Save.

2 In the Export PDF dialog box, select Smallest File Size from the Adobe PDF Preset pop-up menu. Select Acrobat 6 or higher from the Compatibility pop-up menu if your presentation contains multimedia objects like sounds or movies that you also want to export. *(See illustration on next page.)*

3　In the Include area of the General panel of the dialog box, check Hyperlinks and Interactive Elements. Choose Embed All from the Multimedia pop-up menu.

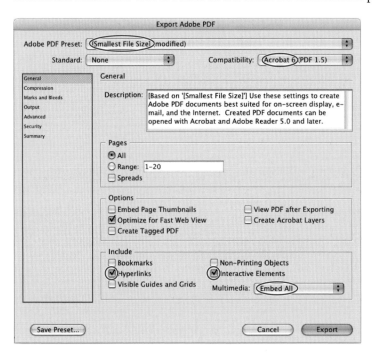

4　Click Export.

 Open the generated PDF with Adobe Acrobat (or the free Adobe Reader) and notice how the pointer changes its appearance when moved over the hyperlink area. Clicking the link on any page of the presentation should cause it to jump directly to page 2 (which looks the same for now as all the other pages, containing only the master page elements).

Navigating through documents

Adobe Acrobat 7.0 Professional and Adobe Reader offer various ways to navigate through a PDF document.

To go directly to a page, a quick way is to use the navigation controls in the status bar at the bottom of the document window. There you can jump to the first, previous, next, and last pages of a document, or you can enter a specific page number.

If you prefer using the menu, you have the same functionality available under View > Go To. The left and right arrow keys on your keyboard are shortcuts to go to the previous and the next page, respectively.

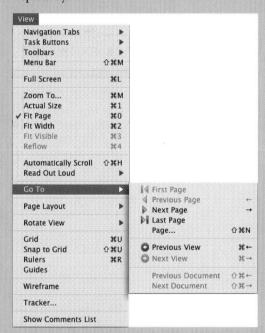

(Continued on next page.)

The command View > Toolbars > Navigation shows the Navigation bar.

The Pages tab in the Navigation pane (F4), on the left side of your document, shows small versions of the pages. To quickly find a page in your document, you can reduce or enlarge the size of the page thumbnails to see as many pages, or as much detail as you want. Double-clicking a page thumbnail opens that page in the main document window.

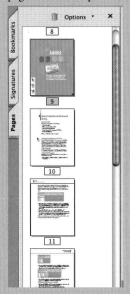

Within a page, you can zoom in and out using the Zoom toolbar (or the Tools > Zoom menu). If you zoom in and can't see the complete page on the screen anymore, use the Pan & Zoom window to keep the overview.

Bookmarks in a PDF document usually mark chapter or section starts, but they can be created at any location within a document. To browse through your bookmarked document, simply use the Bookmarks tab in the Navigation pane, or choose View > Navigation Tabs > Bookmarks.

To learn shortcut keystrokes for navigation through documents, search for "Keys for moving through a document" in Adobe Acrobat 7.0 Professional Help (Help > Complete Acrobat 7.0 Help).

Completing the presentation

Every page based on the same master page will have the same format, and display the same dummy text. To create your presentation, start at page 1 and overwrite the placeholder text with your own presentation material.

1 Switch back to InDesign.

2 To select page 1 for editing, double-click the page 1 icon in the Pages palette.

3 Ctrl-Shift / Command-Shift click each text frame to enable modifying of the master page elements. Select the Type tool, delete the dummy text and type away.

Guidelines for a Slide Presentation

- **Brevity**
  - · Reduce excessive content to a short list of key messages.
- **Simplicity**
  - · Tables should not be too complex as it is strenuous to concentrate.
  - · Use animation and slide transition effects sparingly to not bore your audience or detract from your message.
- **Consistency**
  - · Use the same typefaces throughout.
  - · Position the titles and logos on the same place on each slide.
  - · Consistency makes information easier to absorb.

4   When done, select File > Export to export the pages as a PDF document. In the Export dialog box, select Adobe PDF as Format and navigate to the Lesson08 folder. Accept **mypresentation.pdf** as file name and click Save. Click OK to overwrite the file if it already exists (make sure you did close the file in Acrobat).

5   In the Export Adobe PDF dialog box, all settings should still be selected as specified earlier in this lesson when you did the quick test cycle with the hyperlink. Click Export.

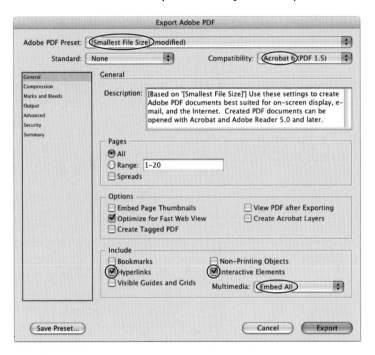

6   Open the exported PDF file in Acrobat and press Command-L / Ctrl-L to switch to Full Screen mode. The arrow keys enable you to move back and forth between the pages (or move forward with each mouse click). Press Command-L again or press the Esc key to get out of the Full Screen mode. In the normal mode, all the usual navigation tools are available to quickly find a specific page.

For the presentation, page transitions can be added in Acrobat (Choose Document > Set Page Transitions). In the Set Transition dialog box you can choose between a lot of different effects and transition speeds, which can be applied to one or more pages of a document. However, it is always better to use those effects sparingly as they can quickly become boring and detract from the message.

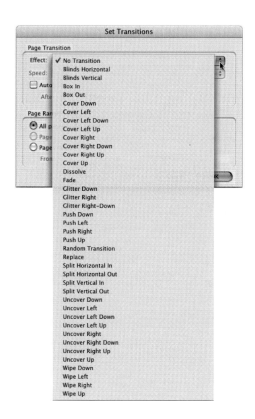

Note: *To give people handouts with a presentation is always a good idea, so they retain the main points. Handouts are also great for those taking notes. Printing from InDesign is a breeze, and, as mentioned before, type will look great.*

Review

▶ **Review questions**

1 What is kerning?

2 If an image and a frame are different sizes, how can you make sure that the proportions of your image will not be altered when you place it into the frame?

3 How can you indent all but the first line of a paragraph?

4 What interactive elements can you add to a presentation created in InDesign?

5 Name three ways to navigate to a specific page in a document.

▶ **Review answers**

1 Kerning means to alter the space between selected pairs of letters to improve legibility and appearance.

2 Choose Object > Fitting > Fit Content Proportionally to scale the image to the required size. There are other commands in InDesign dealing with placing content into a frame. You can center the content within a frame by selecting a graphics frame and choosing Object > Fitting > Center Content; the proportions of both the content and the frame remain unaltered. You can resize the frame to fit its content by choosing Object > Fitting > Fit Frame to Content. There is also the option to change the proportions of the image and keep the frame unchanged, by selecting Object > Fitting > Fit Content to Frame.

3 In the Indents and Spacing section of the Paragraph Style Options dialog box, set a Left Indent for the paragraph, and then a First Line Indent with the negative value of the left indent specified. If you also set a tab stop (in the Tabs section of the Paragraph Style Options dialog box) at the same position as the left indent specified for the paragraph, you can create nicely formatted bullet lists. To do this in your document, type a bullet character followed by a tab character to position the cursor at the same point in each line. InDesign can even take care of entering the bullet and tab character (in the Bullets and Numbering section of the Paragraph Style Options dialog box).

4 InDesign provides a variety of interactive features that can enhance your work: you can insert hyperlinks that let you jump to another location of the document, or add bookmarks that will appear as Bookmark tabs in Acrobat, you can add sound or video clips that can be played in the PDF document, or you can create buttons that perform an action when clicked in Acrobat or Adobe reader.

5 You can go directly to a page by typing a specific page number, using the navigation controls in the status bar. Alternatively, you can use the menu by selecting View > Go To > Page, and entering the page number. You can also click a page thumbnail in the Pages tab in the Navigation pane (View > Navigation Tabs > Pages).

Be prepared for some tinkering when your clients first see your work. But presenting it in Adobe Acrobat PDF means that getting feedback will be a lot easier for everybody.

And when it's time to print out, the PDF file format is great for sending your work to the service provider, and even for making last minute adjustments.

9 Submitting Work for Review

Lesson overview

In this lesson, you'll learn how to do the following:

- Convert an InDesign document to PDF for review.
- Distinguish between email- and browser-based reviews.
- Look at security settings.
- Set up an email-based review in Acrobat.
- Participate in a review, make comments, and indicate text changes.
- Collect and review comments.
- Track reviews.
- Use the TouchUp Text tool.

This lesson should take less than an hour to complete.

In Lesson 1, you set up a folder called CS2CIB Lessons on your hard disk. For this lesson, copy the Lesson09 folder from the *Adobe Creative Suite 2 Classroom in a Book* CD into the CS2CIB Lessons folder.

Adobe Acrobat 7.0 Professional, which comes with Adobe Creative Suite 2, can be used to make the review process a lot easier. In this lesson, the CD cover you created in Lesson 2 will be taken through a typical client review process: setting up an email-based review, sending the piece to the client as a PDF document, commenting on it with note and mark-up tools, and, finally, collecting those comments. You'll even learn how to save the job (and the relationship with your client) from disaster, by making last minute changes with the TouchUp Text tool.

Saving the file for online review

First, your work needs to get saved as a PDF file, which ensures that the client will see everything exactly as you want it to be seen. To do this, start InDesign and open the document you want to send out for a review.

1 In InDesign, open the file CD Cover Final.indd, in the Lesson09 folder, inside the CS2CIB Lessons folder.

For an on screen review, all images can be downsampled to low resolution to reduce the file size, and colors converted to RGB color mode. Since the document contains transparency, the Document's Transparency Blend Space needs to be set to RGB before exporting as PDF. Do not save those changes in the original CD Cover Final.indd, as this will ultimately be printed using the CMYK color mode.

2 Choose Edit > Transparency Blend Space > Document RGB.

3 Choose File > Export. In the Export dialog box, navigate to the Lesson09 folder. Select Adobe PDF from the Format pop-up menu, and enter **CD Cover Review.pdf** as the file's name. Click Save.

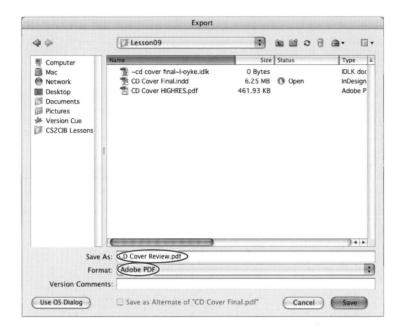

The Export Adobe PDF dialog box will come up. If sending out a document for comments, it's usually all right to send just a low-resolution version of the document. This will enable your clients to see enough to be able to comment, without you having to email them a document that's several megabytes in size. Choosing the right compression options reduces the file size, while still providing enough image detail for those reviewing the material.

4   Select [Smallest File Size] from the Adobe PDF Preset pop-up menu. Choose Acrobat 7 (PDF 1.6) from the Compatibility pop-up menu. *(See illustration on next page.)* Click Export.

Note: In general, when exporting to PDF it is advisable to choose the most recent Acrobat/PDF compatibility level, unless there is a specific need for backward compatibility. Most PDF files created with Acrobat 7 (PDF 1.6) compatibility can still be opened with Acrobat 4.0 and Acrobat Reader 4.0, however, features specific to later versions may be lost or not viewable. For a comparison of the different compatibility settings, search for "PDF compatibility levels" in the Adobe Help Center under Help for InDesign.

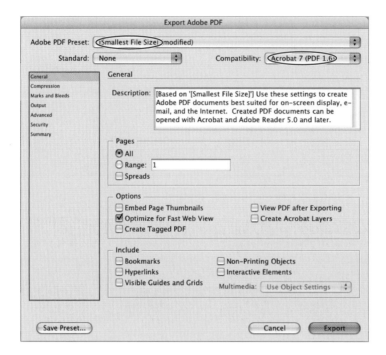

Now the PDF file has a very small file size, while still providing a good quality preview.

Securing a Document

Access to a PDF document can be limited through the following security features, specified when exporting the PDF format:

• A password.

• Encryption, so that only specified users can view the document.

• Server-based security policies, which are especially useful if you want to provide access for a limited time only.

There are two kinds of passwords: a Document Open (user) password and a Permissions (master) password. With a Document Open password, the password must be entered before the document will open. The Permissions password allows you to change the security settings of a document.

When exporting a PDF document, you can specify the security settings in the Security panel of the Export Adobe PDF dialog box.

As an additional security measure, the authenticity of a document can be confirmed with the author's digital signature.

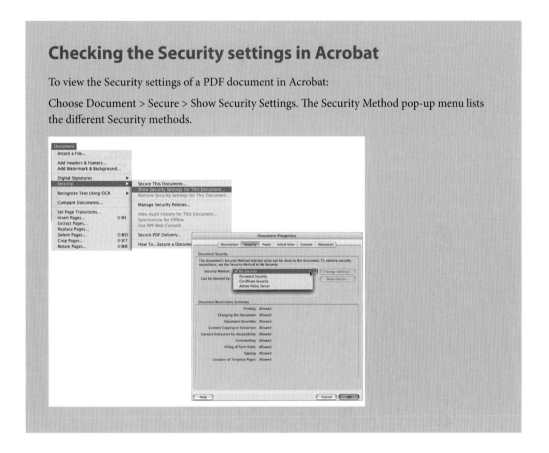

Checking the Security settings in Acrobat

To view the Security settings of a PDF document in Acrobat:

Choose Document > Secure > Show Security Settings. The Security Method pop-up menu lists the different Security methods.

Setting up an email-based review

With Acrobat 7 Professional, you have more control during a document review cycle. This application provides tools for managing a list of reviewers, tracking the review status and sending reminder messages if necessary, inviting additional reviewers to join in later, and generally making the process of giving and receiving feed-back a lot easier. For example, when opening the review document, Acrobat will automatically display clear step-by-step instructions on how to participate in a review process.

Furthermore, it offers the choice between an email- or browser-based review. Browser-based reviews are more interactive because all of the reviewers can see each other's comments. However, a file server has to be set up to host the file and make it accessible to all the reviewers.

In this lesson, you'll learn how to send the PDF file as an attachment to an email. This PDF file becomes the master file in which the comments of the reviewers are incorporated. The initiator of the review can easily track the status of the review process, because each reviewer receives a tracked copy of the document.

Note: *For participating in a review, the use of Acrobat 7.0 and Adobe Reader 7.0 are necessary; some of the commenting tools and features are not available in earlier versions. Adobe Reader 7.0 allows you to add comments to a PDF document, but only if Adobe Acrobat 7.0 Professional was used to enable this feature in the document.*

To initiate the review, do the following:

1   Start Acrobat, and open the file CD Cover Review.pdf in the Lesson09 folder.

2   Select File > Send for Review > Send by Email for Review.

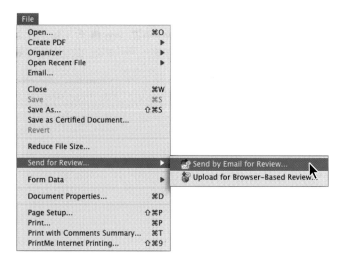

If this is the first time you are using this feature, you need to set up your identity in the Identity Setup dialog box.

3 Enter personal information in the Identity Setup dialog box and click Complete.

Note: *Acrobat requires you to provide a valid email address in the Identity Setup dialog box, so other participants will be able to recognize your invitation.*

4 Choose the file CD Cover Review.pdf from the pop-up menu in the Getting Started panel of the Send by Email for Review dialog box, and then click Next.

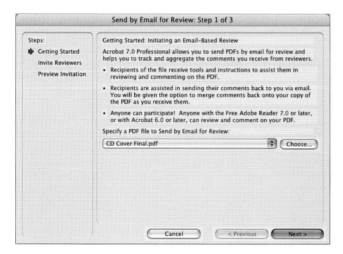

5 Enter the email addresses of the reviewers in the Invite Reviewers panel of the Send by Email for Review dialog box. Make sure to insert a comma, semicolon, or return between each email address. *(See illustration on next page.)*

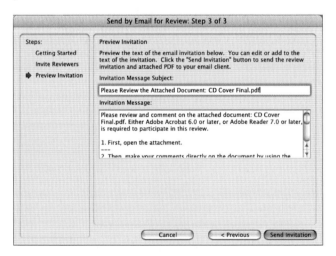

6   Click the Customize Review Options button, and make sure that the option Also allow users of the Free Adobe Reader 7.0 to participate in this review is selected. Click OK to return to the previous panel and then Next to preview the invitation.

7   Read the default email message Acrobat prepared for you. You can modify the text if you wish. Click the Send Invitation button to start the review process.

Acrobat will create in your default email application an outgoing email with the PDF document as an attachment. If the email client is not configured to automatically send messages, it might be necessary to manually click the send button in the email application to send the file.

Adding comments in a review

Let's assume you have been invited to participate in an email-based review, and have just received the email message with the PDF attachment. At the bottom of this message there is a text link to a free download of Adobe Reader.

This next step shows how to add a comment to the original PDF file—this way you don't have to rely upon being able to send emails during the lesson. A comment generally refers to a note, stamp, or mark-up to be contributed to a review. Those comments can be placed anywhere within the document, they can be grouped together, come in different styles, and can even be created as customized stamps.

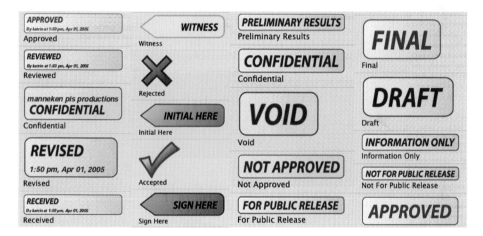

The most frequently used comment comes in form of a note. To create a note, do the following:

1   Open the CD Cover Review.pdf in Acrobat 7.0 or Acrobat Reader 7.0 (double-clicking the attachment in an email would automatically launch the relevant application).

2   Go to Comments > Show Commenting Toolbar.

3   Select the Note tool, and click at the end of the list on the left hand side of the CD Cover.

4   Type **add "Branding"** in the pop-up window. Note that the size of the pop-up window can be adjusted by dragging the lower right corner.

You can close the pop-up window by clicking the Close icon in the top right corner. Clicking (Windows) or double-clicking (Mac OS) the note icon opens the pop-up window again, ready to edit the comment.

Closing the pop-up window will not delete a note. To delete a note, select the note icon, and then press Delete. Alternatively, you can choose Delete from the Options menu in the top right corner of the pop-up window. This menu also gives you access to the Note Properties dialog box where you can change to your liking the color and other aspects of the note's appearance.

Marking up documents

The document can also be marked up with tools from the Drawing Markups toolbar. These enable you to draw circles and other shapes to make the comment more precise. Probably the most natural way to make comments on a printed paper is to take a pen and to scribble away. Acrobat's Pencil tool is the equivalent for marking up PDF documents.

1 If necessary, choose Comments > Show Drawing Markups Toolbar. Select the Pencil tool from the pop-up menu in the Drawing Markups toolbar.

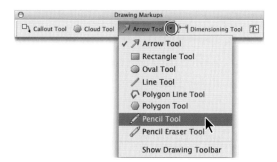

2 With the Pencil tool, draw a big circle around the entire text block on the left. Then draw a little arrow indicating that this block should move further to the left.

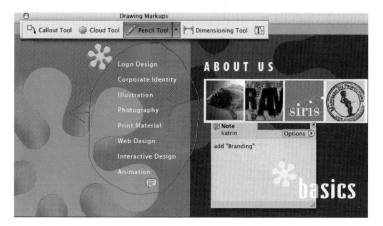

3 Use the Note tool, click next to the arrow, and then type **Move text block 1 inch to left** in the pop-up window to provide more details. *(See illustration on next page.)*

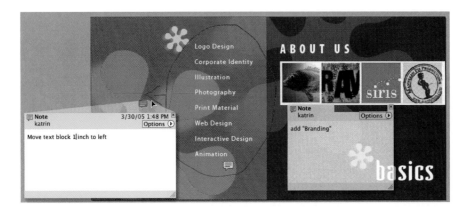

4   Finally, had you received this PDF as an email attachment as part of an email-based review, you could simply click Send Comments in the Commenting toolbar (Comments > Show Commenting Toolbar) to send you comments back to the initiator of the review.

Note: The Send Comments button does not appear on the Commenting toolbar when you are working with an untracked PDF document.

Tracking comments

Now that you understand how to initiate a review, and how to participate by adding comments, it's time to learn how to collect and track those comments, assuming you were the initiator of a review. Since the tracked PDF document contains information about who is the initiator and the participants of the review, Acrobat can behave differently depending on where the document is opened.

Note: If you don't have email access during your lesson, you might not be able to reproduce the following steps, but you can still learn about the process from the illustrations provided.

If you were the initiator of a review and just received comments via email, you would see the following dialog box when double-clicking the attachment to the mail:

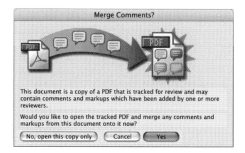

1   To continue, click Yes.

Once the file is open, you can clearly distinguish the merged comments, which you can sort by author, page, date or status.

2   Choose View > Navigation Tabs > Comments to open the Comments panel in the lower part of the window. Here you can review one comment at a time in a list, without fearing that you might overlook something on a page full of comments.

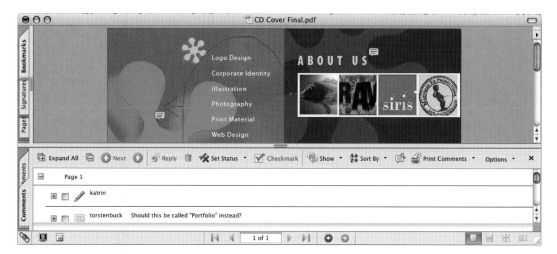

Use the Tracker for managing and tracking the addresses and reviews.

3   Choose Comments > Tracker.

4   In the left pane of the Tracker window, select My Reviews to view the PDF reviews you initiated, or select Participant Reviews to view the PDF documents with the comments you received. *(See illustration on next page.)*

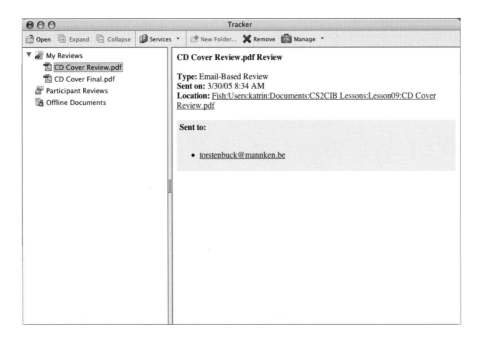

By clicking an email link on the right pane, you can send an email to an individual participant of the review. If you want to send a review reminder to all participants in a review, Right-click / Control-click the icon of the tracked PDF document under My Reviews, and then choose Send Review Reminder from the pop-up menu.

There is much more to learn about managing reviews using the Tracker. To get started, search for "Managing reviews using the Tracker" in Adobe Acrobat 7.0 Professional Help (Help > Complete Acrobat 7.0 Help).

Last minute touch-up in Acrobat

After incorporating all the comments and finalizing the CD cover design, the document can be sent as a PDF file to an output service provider for printing. This time, the images should not be downsampled when exporting the file as PDF, but the [Press Quality] preset should be used. To see how the Touch-up Text tool works, simply use the file CD Cover HIGHRES.pdf provided in the Lesson09 folder for the following steps.

Once the printer receives the PDF file, he'll simply be able to open the file in Acrobat, and print it. You can tell your client that the file is now with the printer, and that you're going on vacation. The end? Alas, no. Apparently your client now needs one more little change. Unfortunately, you're away at the beach, and the printer has neither the original InDesign file, nor the Photoshop file, only the PDF file. Luckily, Acrobat allows some editing directly in the PDF file.

Suppose the text on the front cover of the CD is to be changed to PORTFOLIO rather than ABOUT US. The printer can open the file in Acrobat and edit the text.

1　Open the file CD Cover HIGHRES.pdf in Acrobat 7.0

2　Choose Tools > Advanced Editing > TouchUp Text Tool.

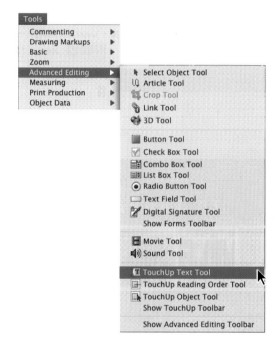

3　Click the text ABOUT US. Acrobat will take a moment to load some system fonts, then display a frame around these words and place a blinking text cursor where you clicked the text. *(See illustration on next page.)*

4   Select the entire text and then type **PORTFOLIO**.

5   To increase the spacing between the characters to better match the original design, select the entire text, and then Right-click / Control-click the text and choose Properties from the pop-up menu. In the TouchUp Properties dialog box, increase the Character Spacing to **0.25**, and then click Close.

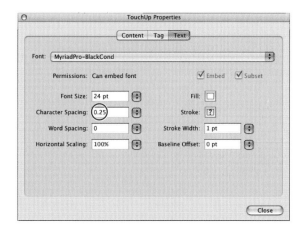

6   Choose File > Deselect All to see the result.

This was easy! Adobe Acrobat Professional can not only simplify the review process, but also put everything together in a convenient format for the printer. And yet it's flexible enough to allow for the changes that clients request at the last minute. That makes it a lifesaver at every stage of the design process.

Note: *Those last minute changes in Acrobat are only a last resort. Although the editing capabilities in Acrobat are quite powerful, you don't have the same control over the text appearance nor access to the full range of OpenType features that you do in InDesign.*

Review

▶ **Review questions**

1 What does the PDF preset Smallest File Size do?

2 Which kinds of passwords can be used to limit access to a PDF document?

3 What do you need before you can initiate a browser-based review?

4 How can a comment be deleted?

5 What does the TouchUp Text tool allow you to do?

▶ **Review answers**

1 The PDF export preset Smallest File Size saves your document to be displayed on the Web or an intranet, or to be send as an email attachment. It downsamples and compresses your document images, resulting in a smaller file size. All colors are converted to RGB. Smallest File Size documents can be opened in Acrobat 5.0 and Acrobat Reader 5.0 or later.

2 The Document Open password, where a password must be entered to open a document, and the Permissions password that allows changes to the security settings of a document.

3 The participants of a browser-based review must have shared access to a server.

4 To delete a comment, you need to click the note icon, and then press Delete. Alternatively, you can Right-click / Control-click the note icon, and then choose Delete from the pop-up menu. Another option—not mentioned in the lesson—is to select the Comments tab, select the comment you wish to delete from the list, and then click the Delete icon. Where comments have been placed on top of each other, using the Comments List is the best way to select specific comments to be deleted. Comments of other reviewers cannot be deleted.

5 The TouchUp Text tool enables you to make some minor, last minute changes to an Adobe PDF document. With this tool, you can edit single letters or do other minor editing. However, if there is more substantial revision to be done, you should edit the original document and generate a new PDF file. You can also

work on only those pages that need revision, and when finished, insert them into the PDF document. It is worth noting that in order to edit text in your PDF document, the font must be either installed on your system or embedded in the document.

Understanding Adobe Version Cue CS2

Overview

Creative professionals face a variety of challenges as they turn out project after project and deal with client demands—all under deadlines that are becoming more and more stringent. While software applications offer all kinds of creative tools and productivity-boosting features, there are still many hurdles to overcome to efficiently manage the design process.

Enter Adobe® Version Cue® CS2, the innovative file manager that's part of Adobe Creative Suite 2. Version Cue lets designers track files from within the familiar Adobe design environment, managing changes and preserving iterations of files for individuals as well as for workgroups. Thumbnail previews let designers find the right file at a glance, or designers can search for files by such specifics as author and keyword. A team of designers can see which files co-workers have open and see when files are completed without leaving their design tools. Version Cue even lets designers search the text of version comments to help them find their files. Additionally, Adobe PDF-based reviews can be managed and tracked easily.

A professional's creative processes and the ability to finish jobs on time and on budget are what matter most. Here are some examples of roadblocks in productivity that can affect profitability:

- A graphic artist losing minutes or hours over the course of a project opening large image files just to see if they are the most current version to edit

- An art director handing off a project from one designer to another, requiring the second designer to embark on a frustrating search for files whose names aren't easily understood because the file-naming convention was either not followed or unique to the original designer

- A layout artist attempting to place an illustration or photo, only to find that it's in use by someone else and cannot be opened

- A creative director losing hard work when her file is overwritten by another designer and having to re-create the work

- A designer trying to consolidate comments and feedback from clients and managers from a variety of faxes, e-mail messages, and hard proofs

This white paper is intended for graphic designers, art directors, freelancers, production managers, web designers, marketing professionals, print and prepress professionals, and others who are involved in the day-to-day, hands-on creation of graphic materials for print and the web. Whether they work alone or in a group, these creative professionals can improve the way they manage their files by learning how to use Version Cue. This paper explains not only how Version Cue works but also how to set up and test Version Cue before integrating it into a workflow. This paper also provides a detailed discussion of the technology's infrastructure. By providing this in-depth look at Version Cue from both productivity and technological viewpoints, this paper seeks to demonstrate how easy Version Cue is to use and to reduce fears and apprehensions that may be associated with implementing a new technology.

The Adobe Creative Suite vision

Adobe understands how designers work and recognizes that time spent on project management takes away from time they would need to spend doing other things—being creative, promoting their businesses, billing out their work—a variety of activities that businesses must engage in to be more profitable. Today's design applications have a broad range of valuable creative features (such as filters, transforms, effects, type choices and controls). Version Cue is one example of how technology can let creative professionals manage information about their assets (current and past versions of a file as well as its metadata) to get better control over their workflow: it enables professionals to find files more quickly, make fewer errors, and use files more efficiently. And as a result of better processes, designers can have more successful businesses.

Integrating this kind of technology within the toolset of Adobe Creative Suite, users can experience the advantages of an improved workflow without switching context or leaving their familiar Adobe design applications.

Adobe Bridge

Adobe has redefined integration with Adobe Bridge, which serves as a connection to each of the applications within Adobe Creative Suite. Designers can browse through and preview any kind of file (even multiple-page PDF files), can run automation scripts and powerful searches, and can synchronize settings across all Adobe Creative Suite components at once—all within the familiar Adobe workspace. Additionally, Bridge serves as a dashboard to important information on files, tips and tricks, and news feeds.

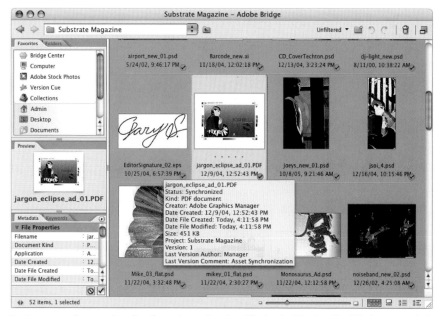

Designers can browse thumbnail previews of project files in the Version Cue Workspace and view information about the contents of each file.

Bridge exposes the power of Version Cue by enabling users to manage their projects easily and experience the advantages of a managed workflow. Using Version Cue and Bridge, users have access to vital workflow information, including the current status of a file (such as who is currently editing the file, or whether a file is the latest version), thumbnails and previews of the different historical versions and alternates for a file, and information about the content of the file.

Metadata

With today's hard drives becoming larger and filled with more and more digital files, it is harder to locate files. Designers waste valuable time as they copy large files from servers, only to open them and realize that they copied the wrong ones. Version Cue, in combination with Bridge, gives users access to metadata—extra text-based information—for each of their files. Some examples of metadata are the author of the file, creation or modification dates and times, version comments, keywords, and image colorspace and resolution settings. All of the component applications of Adobe Creative Suite 2 give users the ability to manually add metadata to a file through a File Info dialog box. Certain kinds of metadata are also automatically added to files as they are saved, such as a list of fonts or colors used in an Adobe InDesign® CS2 file. Bridge also allows users to add and edit file metadata without having to open the file. Additionally, Bridge enables users to automate the appending of metadata to multiple files by using scripts.

PDF-based reviews

More and more designers are seeing the benefit of an all-digital workflow. Adobe PDF files of designs and layouts can be instantly generated and distributed via e-mail for review. However, managing such a review process—coordinating it, communicating its presence, aggregating the comments from multiple reviewers, and integrating it within the design workflow—is a complex task. Version Cue offers a fully integrated PDF-based review process that enables users to distribute PDF files, track comments and manage review cycles.

Users begin by creating a PDF file from within any Adobe Creative Suite component, and then launch the Version Cue CS2 Review feature from the Version Cue Administration utility. There, users can easily manage PDF-based reviews by creating new review cycles, participating in reviews that they've been invited to, and perform other review-related tasks. As reviewers make comments by using the review features in Adobe Acrobat®, the designer can track and respond to those comments.

Adobe Acrobat 7.0 Professional gives users the ability to activate functionality in a PDF file that will allow others with Adobe Reader 7 to participate in a review. Once a PDF file is created and opened in Acrobat Professional, the designer can choose Enable for Commenting in Adobe Reader from the Comments menu. The designer can then use the PDF-based review functionality mentioned above to include those using the free Adobe Reader.

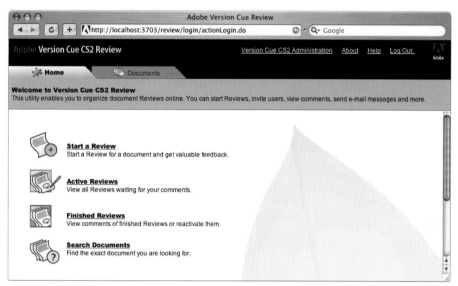

With the Adobe Version Cue CS2 Review feature, users can easily manage the PDF review process.

Version Cue and enhanced productivity

First, this article looks at the key productivity features and benefits of Version Cue. Version Cue offers benefits to individual designers as well as groups working in a collaborative environment.

Powerful file management for individual users

Version Cue offers individual designers a powerful way to manage the files they work on every day. Version Cue streamlines the process of creating both historical versions and alternates for files, maintaining a file history, locating and managing files, and backing up or restoring entire projects. Benefits to individual users are:

• **Efficient file management** As clients request changes to files, designers can create historical versions of both Adobe and non-Adobe files and track the changes made throughout the project. At any time, designers can view these versions and even promote older versions of files to become the current version. Version Cue displays the status of a file either in Bridge or directly from within any Adobe Creative Suite component. Version Cue also prevents designers from accidentally overwriting past versions while they work.

Streamlined File Management and Access

• Historical versioning within the CS2 versions of Adobe Photoshop®, Illustrator, InDesign, and Adobe GoLive®*

• Thumbnail previews

• Ability to track non-Adobe files

• On-demand metadata when opening files

• Search on version comments, keywords, author, and other file information

• Enhanced link management

• Web-based review of PDF project files

Improved File Sharing

• Alerts and prompts guide users through potential conflicts

• IDs, permissions, and restrictions can be applied

• Projects are saved in a single workspace

Ease of Use

• Out-of-the-box functionality

• Local or remote user-based file-serving

• Optional expert administrative controls

* Users of Adobe InCopy® CS2, a separate product not included in Adobe Creative Suite, can also access a Version Cue workspace— which is available only as part of Adobe Creative Suite—if there is at least one copy of Adobe Creative Suite. InCopy CS2 workflows will not be covered in this white paper.

Alternates Designers can create alternates of their design files, which might be variations of a design based on prior versions; or could be designated from completely different photos for different editions of a publication, for example. Version Cue makes it easy to manage variations of a design. Designers can access alternates from Bridge or even swap between them directly from the Links palette within either InDesign or Adobe Illustrator®, making it simple to present a variety of design ideas to clients and creative directors.

- **Sharing** Designers can share files easily either with or without a server. Version Cue also offers guidance to users so that files can be safely shared without collision.

- **Search capabilities** Designers can find files quickly by searches based on file metadata, which designers can add to files as they save versions and alternates.

- **Review by external parties** Designers can create PDF files, manage review, and easily set up access privileges.

- **Archiving** Designers can easily manage the backup and archiving of design projects. Designers can also retrieve projects that have already been archived. Additionally, the entire Version Cue Workspace can be backed up on a regular schedule using the Version Cue Administration utility.

- **Administration** Version Cue is configured to work efficiently using the default settings. More advanced users can customize settings to meet their needs through the included advanced settings administration utility.

Workflow enhancements for collaborative users

In addition to all of the benefits that individual users enjoy, Version Cue lets workgroups easily share projects and safely collaborate on files by providing information about shared state, usage and edit conflicts, and resolution of these conflicts. Additionally, Version Cue can be set up to perform in either a user-based or a server-based configuration. Benefits to collaborative users are:

- Managed PDF-based reviews. Version Cue manages the complex content-approval process by allowing users to initiate and participate in PDF-based review cycles. By tracking comments from multiple reviewers in a central location, users can respond to the comments of other viewers in a truly collaborative fashion.

- Simplified file organization and access. Version Cue provides a projects-centered workspace where designers can organize related files and separate private and collaborative projects. Individuals can install their workspaces on their own computers; designers working on teams can allow colleagues to access their workspaces as desired, without the need to purchase, install, and configure additional hardware and software. Thumbnail previews provide visual cues to file content, and files can be searched on information such as author, keyword, and date.

- Secure and reliable collaboration. Designers can collaborate transparently on projects. They can be confident that everyone is using the correct file version without slowing down other team members. Multi-user access makes files available to designers, compositors, and managers, while guidance messages and alerts prevent files from being accidentally overwritten.

Alerts and guidance: If someone in the workgroup opens a file that's already in use, Version Cue displays guides to minimize editing conflicts (top) and displays an "in use" message in the title bar (bottom).

A typical Version Cue environment

As mentioned earlier, Version Cue uses a project Workspace to store file versions as well as information about files. When a designer installs Adobe Creative Suite, a Version Cue Workspace is automatically and by default placed on that individual's computer. The designer who works independently and doesn't need to share files is already set up, and the designer who is part of a workgroup is ready to use Version Cue in a user-based implementation.

In a user-based implementation, Version Cue projects and files are shared directly from a designer's local hard drive; a standalone server is not required. The individual who sets up a project essentially serves it to team members. Anyone who is networked to that individual's computer and has Adobe Creative Suite; the CS2 versions of Photoshop, Illustrator, InDesign, or GoLive or Acrobat 7.0 Professional; or any application that supports the standard Web Distributed Authoring and Versioning (WebDAV) protocol can access the files. (For more on WebDAV, see "Use of standards," page 7.) A user-based implementation is the easiest and most affordable way to implement Version Cue, saving workgroups from buying and configuring a dedicated server to run the system.

A server-based implementation may provide benefits for more structured workgroups. In a user-based implementation, files are accessible to teams only as long as the computer where the project resides is turned on and networked to the group. In some situations—for example, when a designer works remotely and is only sporadically connected to the network—a user-based implementation isn't expedient. For workgroups that need 24/7 availability and perhaps greater storage capacity and network bandwidth, Version Cue can be configured to run from a dedicated server or even a central computer being used as a server (no special server operating system is required). One Version Cue Workspace may be installed for each licensed instance of Adobe Creative Suite. The Workspace may be installed on an individual designer's computer or on a central server as desired, depending on the needs of the studio or production environment.

When projects are complete and their assets are no longer required, designers can export projects from the Version Cue Workspace and archive them on external hard drives or servers. This archival process allows designers to keep the Version Cue Workspace lean and not congest their hard drives with unnecessary files.

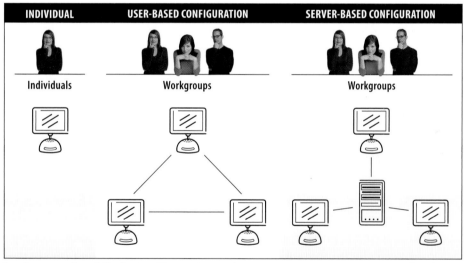

Local or server-based file sharing: Version Cue can be set up to operate in a user- or server-based networked environment. In a user-based implementation, files and projects are shared from an individual's own hard drive. In a server-based environment, the Version Cue Workspace resides on a separate computer.

Version Cue versus traditional file-management systems

There is a variety of traditional solutions for managing files and versions, but all have similar limitations: they're good for structured environments but tend to be hard to learn or take too much effort to use, so designers get frustrated and either make inadvertent mistakes or give up; these systems are external to the design environment, so the user has to switch context to check assets in and out of the system (reserving or locking the file).

Version Cue, in contrast, fits naturally into Adobe creative professional workflows, providing greater flexibility and ease of use so that designers can continue to work as they always have and yet also enjoy the benefits of file version management—without extra expense or interrupting routine production tasks. This is because Version Cue manages the process as well as the assets.Following are several solutions that are being used today in traditional environments and the ways in which Version Cue offers added value.

The operating system

The first solution is no file management: designers simply browse an operating system or directory to find the file they need. The operating system (OS) was never meant to meet advanced needs of designers with complex file formats and embedded or placed assets, and this is the least productive way for designers to find what they're looking for. Because they have a minimal amount of file information, designers have to open the file to figure out what it is.

In contrast, Version Cue users access files from within Bridge, which offers the ability to view file thumbnails and pertinent metadata, all without leaving the familiar Adobe interface environment. Additionally, designers working in an Adobe Creative Suite component can choose File > Open and click the Use Adobe Dialog button. An enhanced capabilities window appears, displaying (by user choice) either a text list or thumbnail previews of all available project files. Thumbnails are accompanied by tool tips that contain a summary of significant file information, such as the name of the last person to work on the file and comments describing what the person did in the most recent iteration. Designers can also locate a file easily by searching on such information as version comments, author, keyword, and date directly in this window. This file information is stored as industry-standard Extensible Metadata Platform (XMP) metadata. *(For more on XMP, see "Use of standards" sidebar.)*

Use of Standards

Version Cue is built on several open industry standards that enhance its core functionality. Among these standards are XMP and WebDAV—two acronyms that are used liberally throughout this white paper. What do they mean?

• XMP: XMP, which stands for Extensible Metadata Platform, is based on World Wide Web Consortium (W3C®) standards and is available via open source license. It is an enabling technology that adds intelligence to files so that they're easier to find, reuse, archive, and exchange. Supported by all Adobe native file formats, including Adobe PDF, XMP lets designers capture, preserve, and share meaningful Extensible Markup Language (XML)-based metadata across files and workflows, opening the door for more efficient job processing, workflow automation, and efficient rights management, among other possibilities.

Version Cue automatically embeds XMP metadata, such as author, date, title, description, and keywords, when designers save versions of files. Designers can also add XMP file information in the File Info dialog boxes of Adobe CS applications. Comments that are added manually by designers when they save versions are also managed by Version Cue as metadata. Thus, designers can quickly locate a file in a Version Cue project by searching XMP-based version comments, keywords, copyright information, authors, and titles.

• WebDAV: Another standard that Version Cue uses is WebDAV, or Web Distributed Authoring and Versioning. WebDAV, which is administered by the Internet Engineering Task Force (IETF), is a protocol that facilitates collaborative content creation in a platform- and technology-independent environment, and makes it easier to reuse content and share knowledge collaboratively over the web. Within Adobe Creative Suite, Version Cue uses a richer protocol, but Version Cue uses WebDAV to enable applications other than the CS and CS2 versions of Photoshop, Illustrator, and InDesign to communicate with the Version Cue workspace. Version Cue also acts as a WebDAV client to enable the importing and exporting of content to and from a WebDAV server.

File-naming conventions

A second solution is to devise a file-naming convention that can (hopefully) be understood and used by everyone in a workgroup. But file-naming conventions are cumbersome: They are often intuitive only to the person who created the system, and they require more discipline than many designers have time to sustain. If the file-naming convention is not rigorously followed, multiple versions can easily circulate among a team, with no mechanism to ensure that the most current version is always used and not accidentally overwritten.

When Version Cue is part of a workflow, file-naming conventions become a nonissue because designers rely on thumbnails and metadata to find the files they are looking for. It is no longer necessary to use a Save As to save a new version of an asset. When a designer opens a file, a working copy of the most recent version of the project file is created on the hard drive; new versions are eventually saved back to the Version Cue Workspace from these working copies. If someone opens a file that's already in use, Version Cue alerts the designer and identifies the other person who is using the file. Version Cue continues to provide helpful guidance to both users so that they are aware of the impact of their actions on each other's work, allowing groups to collaborate more efficiently and helps ensure that everyone uses the correct versions of files.

After making changes to the file, designers choose File > Save A Version to save it back to the Version Cue Workspace, along with any comments that may make it easier to find the right file or to track changes later or alert others about what has happened in this version. Additional metadata is also automatically captured in the file, including user name, date, and time.

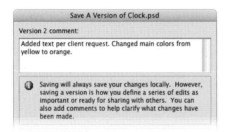

Save versions: Choose File > Save A Version to save files back to the Version Cue Workspace, adding such version comments as a description of the edits that were made.

Third-party tools

Alternatively, designers can use a third-party tool that catalogs files, provides previews, and perhaps offers search capabilities. However, these products generally require scripting to connect to designers' everyday applications. Or creative teams can use mainstream databases to catalog their files. Unfortunately, these databases typically entail a relatively complex level of programming to connect to a creative or publishing workflow. They can also be difficult to scale depending on the implementation, and often require regular system administration. As a result, third-party tools and ad hoc scripted solutions can be a hassle and are too expensive for many design teams to implement and maintain. And because these solutions depend on designers to manually check files in and out of an external system, they're not used consistently and sometimes cause as many workflow problems as they solve.

Version Cue can be used as soon as it's installed; no administrative or user setup is required. Power users, however, can access the kinds of advanced administrative controls that are desirable in more structured environments, such as user access control, project backup, and Workspace maintenance. These controls make Version Cue as robust as necessary for various design and production environments.

Versioning is transparent and implicit in the saving process, requiring no extra steps, applications, or costs. Version Cue lets creative professionals work the way they always have but brings an end to the headaches of devising file-naming conventions and conducting tedious searches across hard drives, networked servers, or File Transfer Protocol (FTP) sites.

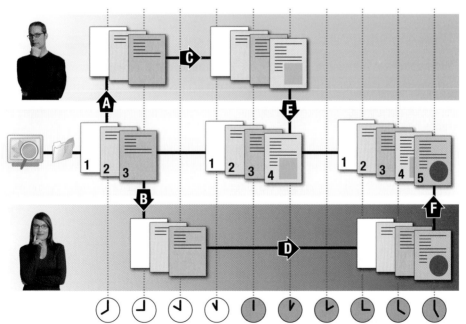

Version Cue workflow: A. Top user opens file from Version Cue Workspace at 8 A.M. B. Bottom user opens same file from Workspace at 9 A.M. C. Top user edits own working copy, choosing Save command to save changes to only his working copy. D. Bottom user edits her own working copy, choosing Save command to save changes to only her working copy. E. Top user chooses Save A Version command to add fourth file version to the Workspace. F. Bottom user chooses Save A Version command to add fifth file version to the Workspace; changes from top user appear only in fourth version.

Custom solutions

Lastly, creative workgroups can opt to set up an FTP or other file server, or implement a customized high-end digital asset management solution. But these solutions are not only expensive, they also need constant maintenance as well as firewalls and other technological support that make them prohibitive for most creative professionals to use.

Version Cue is included with Adobe Creative Suite and therefore requires no additional costs. Because this functionality is built into Photoshop CS2, Illustrator CS2, InDesign CS2, GoLive CS2, and Adobe Acrobat 7.0 Professional directly, IT departments need not worry about additional applications to support or maintain.

Underlying technology and implementation

This section takes a more detailed look at the technological underpinnings of Version Cue and the nuts and bolts of implementing Version Cue in a production workflow.

Understanding Version Cue terminology

Workspaces When using Version Cue to manage, organize, and share files and file information, designers or workgroups must access a Workspace. This Workspace, whose location is defined during the installation process, stores all file versions and the XMP metadata for all files.
(**Note:** The location of the Workspace can be changed at any time, if required.) It also preserves and updates the relationships (links) between files. The Workspace can reside on an individual's hard drive or on a centralized computer or dedicated server.

Designers access the Workspace directly in Bridge, where they can create and connect to their own and others' Workspaces and projects, view project files, and access workgroup commands. In this way, access to project files is integrated into the workflow directly in a common, familiar user interface. Alternatively, users can access Workspaces directly from Open, Save, Save As, and Place dialog boxes in the CS2 versions of Photoshop, Illustrator, and InDesign. GoLive CS2, meanwhile, gives designers access to the Workspace through its Site Manager; indeed, Site Manager acts as a Version Cue project manager because it is the native file-management solution in GoLive for managing links between files. The Site window in GoLive is optimized for handling the many types of assets required to construct a website. By working through the Site Manager, Version Cue enhances GoLive workflows.

Projects A project is a folder in the Version Cue Workspace that contains related files grouped as desired within other folders. Sharing is enabled for entire projects rather than for individual files. Projects can contain any file. Some non-Adobe file types can also be managed and versioned by Version Cue. However, file management and version management in Version Cue will be most robust with the files created by the CS versions of Photoshop, Illustrator, InDesign, and GoLive. Projects can be kept private, even on shared Workspaces, or shared as desired with or without assigning user access privileges. Designers can define one or more projects. For example, a designer could create one project for files that don't need to be shared, another for files that need to be shared by everyone in the group, and a third for files that are to be shared only with colleagues who have appropriate privileges. All shared projects are open and accessible to others with privileges as long the computer hosting the Workspace can be seen on a network. Users who are behind a firewall or connecting via a virtual private network (VPN) will also have access to files in shared projects.

Working copies When a file from a Version Cue project is opened, a working copy is created and when the designer starts editing the file it is marked as "In Use." As designers edit, they can preserve intermediate changes by choosing File > Save, which updates the working copy. When designers decide that the file has reached a new version milestone, they use the updated working copy to create a new version in the Version Cue Workspace by choosing File > Save A Version, at which time the file is marked as "Synchronized" because the working copy and the project version are now the same. By using working copies to edit files, Version Cue helps protect the master project versions from inadvertent, unwanted changes.

Regardless where the Version Cue Workspace is located, by default, working copies are kept on the designer's own hard drive. Working copies of project files are located in a folder for each project that is in a Version Cue folder, which is automatically created inside the designer's My Documents folder (Documents in Mac OS® X). The user is able to relocate working files to any location on a non-networked drive if desired.

Historical versions and alternates Throughout a design project, files go through many iterations or version changes. Historical versions of files are edits or changes that have been made over time. Versions are also important when a designer creates several different design ideas during exploratory design phases. Clients may also ask to see a particular design in a few different ways. Version Cue refers to these kinds of files as alternates, and a designer can easily specify files as being alternates of other files. Through Bridge or from within Illustrator or InDesign layouts, designers can easily replace or swap out alternate versions of their design files.

Alternates can be helpful in a review process as well, offering design choices. Files with completely different content can also be designated as alternates. This may be of use in publications with different editions, or different languages. Alternates can also be used for lo-res/hi-res images when working with web and print usages of a document. To contrast the two concepts, a historical version can be thought of as a snapshot in time and an alternate a parallel path in the design process.

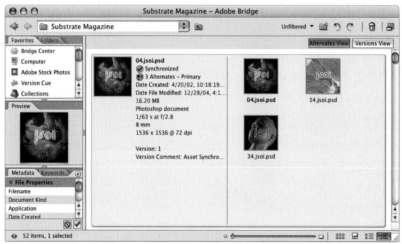

Alternates. Designers can easily manage alternative designs directly within Illustrator and Photoshop layouts, as well as see a listing of alternates in Bridge.

Multi-user access With working copies of project files, Version Cue enables multiple designers to access and work on a file. For example, if two designers need to access an illustration at the same time (one needs to tweak it, the other needs to design a layout and needs to print the illustration for example), Version Cue automatically lets each one edit a working copy of the most recent version. The second designer to access the illustration is informed that the file is already in use and can decide whether to continue working with it. This process helps ensure that everyone's access to project files is flexible and enables workflows to progress when more than one designer needs to work on the same file. In this scenario, however, each designer's working file won't incorporate changes made by the other. When each designer finishes editing a file, he or she may save a new version with his or her unique changes to the Workspace, and then manually reconcile the differences. Alternatively, the second designer may start a new version thread by saving changes to a new file with the Save As command, or simply wait to make changes until the first designer is finished and the file is no longer in use.

Some workgroups may need to limit the amount of freedom allowed when opening and saving files. The first person who opened the file can be enabled as the only person with rights to save a version. This feature can be activated as needed for any project by turning on the Enable Lock Protection for this Project feature in the Version Cue Administration utility.

In addition to its integration with the components of Adobe Creative Suite, Version Cue can be used with any application that supports WebDAV, including Microsoft Office applications.

Setting up and installing Version Cue

The Version Cue Workspace installs as part of a typical Adobe Creative Suite installation. Alternatively, the Version Cue Workspace can be installed separately, such as on a server. In either case, Version Cue is ready to use immediately—the Workspace is turned on and running by default following installation.

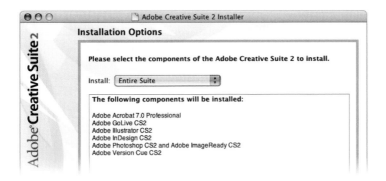

Installation options: Version Cue installs automatically with Adobe Creative Suite. By default, it places a Version Cue Workspace on the individual's hard drive.

Turning Version Cue off and on The Version Cue Workspace is configured via an Administration utility accessible from the Adobe Version Cue CS2 System Preferences. (An icon is also installed and visible in the systray area on Windows® and in the menu bar on Mac OS X, providing a convenient way to reach the Advanced Administration utility as well as Version Cue System Preferences.) The Workspace is automatically turned on after installation, and the option to Turn Version Cue On When The Computer Starts is selected, so Version Cue does not have to be manually restarted every time the computer is turned on.

If designers want or need to share projects in a user-based Workspace implementation, they choose This Workspace Is Visible To Others from the Workspace Access menu. Selecting This Workspace Is Private, alternatively, keeps the designer's Workspace hidden from others on the network. Even when a Workspace is visible to others, projects in that Workspace may be individually designated as private, keeping them hidden from others.

In a user-based Workspace implementation, each designer on the network has control over the projects in his or her own Workspace as well as over the Workspace itself, giving each member of the workgroup both flexibility and control over file sharing. A designer could, for example, temporarily turn off sharing for a project to ensure that no one else accesses a design idea that hasn't been approved by a client, or when design files have been sent out for review and the designer doesn't want them to be accidentally changed. Setting privileges is another way to control access to shared files. (For more on privileges, see "Advanced administration features".)

	USER-BASED	SERVER-BASED
Availability	When computer is on	Server may be offline at times
Capacity	Size of user's hard drive	Usually much larger capacity drives
Network access	When computer is on	Server is usually available
Backup	User's projects are backed up	Entire workgroup's projects are backed up
Performance	Slower if accessed by others	Usually no performance issues

Implementation differences: Some differences between User-based and server-based implementations.

To configure Version Cue to run in a server-based implementation, the Workspace should be installed from the CD directly onto the server's hard drive. A Version Cue Workspace broadcasts its presence on a network, eliminating the need for designers to deal with Internet Protocol (IP) addresses and other configuration settings. (Although servers typically remain on, choosing the option to turn on Version Cue when the computer starts, activates the Workspace automatically if the server does need to be restarted.)

Turning on Version Cue in Adobe Creative Suite components Version Cue is already enabled in each of the Creative Suite 2 components except in Acrobat 7.0 Professional, where the user must explicitly turn on Version Cue functionality by selecting the Enable Version Cue Workgroup File Management check box in the General Preferences dialog box in Acrobat.

By default, Workspace settings in Version Cue are optimized for an individual designer who is working with mixed-media projects and with 128 MB of RAM available to the Workspace. (That means 128 MB of RAM above and beyond the 192 MB of RAM required to run any other single component of Adobe Creative Suite; this is the minimum system requirement to run Version Cue. With modern memory management, this requirement is used dynamically, as when Version Cue is idle, it only uses roughly 30-50 MB of RAM.) A designer or system administrator may increase the amount of memory dedicated to the Version Cue Workspace and optimize it for the anticipated number of people who will be accessing the Workspace. However, in practice, even in large workgroups, more than 256 MB does not need to be specified for Version Cue. These changes are made in the Settings tab of Version Cue System Preferences. Workspaces and projects may be unlimited in size, but there is a 2-GB limit to a single file in a Version Cue project.

Creating projects Once Version Cue is installed and is active both in the OS and in the components of Adobe Creative Suite, designers may create a new Version Cue project. There are several ways to create a project. First, the designer selects the Workspace where the project will be hosted. For an individual, this will be his or her own hard drive. In a workgroup, a project can be created on any visible Workspace that has been shared by others (in a user-based implementation) or on a server (in a server-based implementation).

In Bridge, a designer can choose Tools > Version Cue > New Project, name the project, and add a description. To make the project available to others in a user-based implementation, the designer must select Share This Project With Others. As noted earlier, projects can be unshared at any time. If a server hosts the Workspace, the project is shared by default.

Additionally, a designer can choose File > Open or File > Place in the CS2 versions of Photoshop, Illustrator, or InDesign, click the Use Adobe Dialog button, and choose New Project from the Project Tools menu. Projects can also be created through the GoLive CS site wizard or in Adobe Version Cue Workspace Administration.

Connecting to Version Cue remotely

Having the flexibility and scalability to be used by individual designers, in user-based implementations, and on networked servers is great, but today's production environments are often quite complex. Many designers work remotely—either temporarily or permanently. They may be located in a different branch of the company, such as an international sales office, that's on a separate network. They may go to a client's office for a meeting, work at home for a day, or occasionally use their laptops in the lobby of a convention center or on an airplane. In all of those cases, their work on a Version Cue project does not have to stop. Members of a workgroup can connect remotely to a Version Cue Workspace, access files, edit them, and save versions without slowing down team members.

To connect to a Version Cue project hosted by a Version Cue Workspace that's not on the designer's own subnetwork, the designer uses the Version Cue Client URL or, if he or she is using an application that supports WebDAV, the Version Cue WebDAV Client URL. From the CS version of Photoshop, Illustrator, or InDesign, the designer opens a Version Cue project by choosing File > Open and clicking the Use Adobe Dialog button. In the dialog box that appears, the designer chooses Connect To from the Project Tools menu. (In GoLive CS, the designer chooses File > New Site > Version Cue Project > Connect to Version Cue > Custom Server.) Additionally, the user can use the Connect To feature in Bridge. In wide area network (WAN) environments with firewalls, users will need VPN or alternative access.

Using Workspace Administration, designers in trusted environments or who have appropriate privileges in nontrusted environments can also create and share Version Cue projects remotely and perform administrative tasks.

Using advanced administration features

Additional administrative controls are also available to power users and system administrators.

Trusted versus nontrusted environments By default, Version Cue operates in trusted working environments, which provides the greatest out-of-the-box flexibility to designers because shared files can be accessed without a password. However, there may be designers on a workgroup's network who do not need access to Version Cue projects or who perhaps must be deliberately prevented from accessing files. In magazine publishing, for example, editorial and advertising files may reside on the same network but should be accessible only to their respective departments. For these and other nontrusted environments, system administrators can establish user logins and privileges by using Workspace Administration.

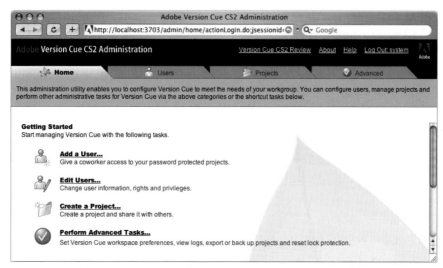

Version Cue Workspace Administration home page: Designers and system administrators can manage IDs and privileges, and perform such maintenance as project backups and exports, by using Workspace Administration.

Accessing Workspace Administration Workspace Administration can be accessed in several ways:

• From Version Cue System Preferences. When Version Cue is turned on, designers can navigate to the Settings tab, and click Advanced Administration.

• From Photoshop, Illustrator, and InDesign by choosing File > Open, clicking the Use Adobe Dialog button, and selecting a Workspace to administer. Designers then choose Tools > Edit Properties and click Advanced Administration.

• From the Site menu in GoLive CS; a site (Version Cue project) must be open for this menu to be available.

• From the icon installed and visible in the systray area on Windows and in the menu bar on Mac OS X. This is a convenient way to reach the Advanced Administration utility as well as Version Cue System Preferences.

When a designer installs a Version Cue Workspace, Version Cue automatically creates a permanent system user login ID with administrator privileges, enabling initial access to the Workspace administration.

Remember, passwords are not required and user accounts do not have to be explicitly created to share Version Cue Workspaces and projects. Designers simply need to be on the same subnetwork or have the Version Cue Workspace IP or Domain Name System (DNS) address and port number to access a shared Workspace across a WAN. To restrict Version Cue projects, however, a system administrator can edit a project's existing user IDs or create new user IDs and assign them to specific projects.

In addition to establishing user IDs, Workspace Administration can be used to manage projects and to apply more stringent controls over file versioning. Lock protection for files can be enabled, restricting file versioning in a multi-user scenario. Once a designer begins editing an available file in a Version Cue project that is lock-protected, only that designer can save the next version of that file to the Version Cue project. Another designer who chooses to edit that file simultaneously won't be able to save changes to a new version of that file, even after the first designer has saved a version. The second designer will have to save changes to a new file or to a new location on the Workspace, or wait to open the newest version of the original file when it becomes available to edit after the first user saves a version. Lock protection for files that are currently in use can be removed through the Advanced page of Workspace Administration. Locks can be deleted for a project, for a particular user, or for the entire Workspace.

Performing maintenance, archiving, and backup

In addition to managing users, privileges, and projects, Workspace Administration can be used to perform maintenance and archive projects. Additionally, users have the ability to schedule regular backups of the entire Workspace, as well as archive individual projects.

Maintenance Maintenance tasks include editing Workspace preferences: making projects or an entire Workspace private or shared, renaming Workspaces, defining log options, and setting default FTP and Hypertext Transfer Protocol (HTTP) proxy servers. In addition, system administrators can delete old file versions from projects, duplicate or delete entire projects, and export and back up projects.

Exporting projects Exporting a Version Cue project creates a copy of that project that contains only the current version of each project file. In other words, exported projects do not include the entire history of each file's versions. Therefore, projects should not be exported as a way to preserve the historical versions of all files within a project; projects should be exported only when the current or final versions of files are necessary, such as for an archive. Exported copies can serve as archives of a project outside of the Version Cue Workspace, or can be delivered as proofs or final files to clients. Version Cue projects can be exported to a different computer via FTP or WebDAV, but Version Cue does not offer connectivity to dedicated third-party archiving systems.

Backing up projects Designers can also create copies of projects that preserve all versions in addition to such information as file comments. By default, backups are stored on the same Version Cue Workspace as the original project, in the Backups folder (although the user can change this location by using the Version Cue CS2 Control Panel). When a designer backs up a project, he or she selects what to include, such as project metadata and file information entered when versions are saved from Adobe Creative Suite components.

It is a good idea to regularly back up Version Cue projects to avoid potential loss of data due to unanticipated system events (backups can be scheduled as well). Designers or administrators can give unique file names to projects, such as projectname_date, so that in the event of data loss or corruption, projects can be restored to their state at a given point in time. Backing up the entire Version Cue Workspace might be more appropriate as it carries basic user login information as well as all project data for all projects. Note that backing up may take significant disk space, because it creates a complete duplicate of all versions of all files.

A designer or system administrator can also back up (and restore) entire Version Cue Workspaces by using the Advanced page of Workspace Administration. Restoring a backup copy of a Version Cue Workspace replaces all current data on the Workspace, including Version Cue projects, files, and versions. Backups of Version Cue Workspaces can be restored only if they were created with the same version of the Version Cue feature that the designer or administrator used.

Handling data corruption

Version Cue handles data corruption in one of three ways, depending on the severity of the problem. First, Version Cue monitors its database and file repository automatically during each Version Cue Workspace start up. If this check detects a problem with file data, Version Cue executes a self-repair routine, automatically and transparently to the designer. As a result, if a problem arises it can be diagnosed and repaired without the designer ever knowing, and without disruption to creative workflows.

If the database becomes corrupted and Version Cue cannot self-repair, then the designer receives an alert that indicates the presence of the problem. The designer is then given the option of running a more robust repair utility that is present in the Workspace environment.

If the self-repair or the repair utility can't resolve the data corruption, the designer or system administrator must manually export all affected Version Cue projects—preserving only current file versions—to a new Workspace. Version Cue does this using a file recovery index. Problems that require the manual export of Version Cue projects have not been reported as of the time this publication was finalized, but Adobe has provided the file recovery index to handle an unforseen problem.

Making Version Cue Work for You

Each workflow presents a variety of demands and challenges, and you may want to think about how Version Cue will also change the way you or your department works. The following information can assist you as you consider adding Version Cue to your workflow.

Testing the system

As with the introduction of any new technology in a working production environment, it is wise to test Version Cue in a limited capacity before rolling it out to an entire workgroup. This process minimizes potentially costly and time-consuming glitches and helps ensure that team members work as smoothly as possible with Version Cue as they integrate it into their daily routines.

Here is one scenario for testing Version Cue that moves slowly. (You may feel more comfortable moving at a more rapid pace with the progress of such a pilot test). To set up a test environment for Version Cue, install it first on a computer that is either not on the network or is not used for daily production or file sharing. Set up the Workspace initially as private (Choose This Workspace Is Private in Version Cue System Preferences). Allow one individual—either the system administrator or an experienced designer or production professional on the team—to experiment with a project. This individual can either create a new blank project for testing purposes or import existing files into a new project by dragging files directly into the project using Bridge. Lastly, a designer can create a project through Workspace Administration. Workspace Administration offers options to import files from a folder, from an FTP site, or from a WebDAV server. (See "Advanced administration features," to learn how to access Workspace Administration, and refer to Version Cue Help for more information about importing and synchronizing files and projects.)

After experimenting with creating projects, adding files, saving versions to Version Cue, and learning how to browse and search for files, the tester can access the Version Cue Workspace from a second computer that has a CS version of Photoshop, Illustrator, InDesign, or GoLive. Then two people can begin to share project and files, familiarize themselves with in-use alerts, and understand how to synchronize working copies of files that multiple users access simultaneously.

After one or two people are familiar with Version Cue, the technology can be phased in to other members of the workgroup and installed on working production systems. As workstations are phased in during the testing period, some files on those computers may be managed by Version Cue and some may not. If desired, the Version Cue Workspace may be turned off and on without affecting the nonmanaged production work on those workstations.

Scaling Version Cue

Version Cue is a scalable technology. It is a straightforward process to migrate from an individual configuration to sharing files in a networked user-based implementation. Designers can make their Workspaces publicly available at any time by using Version Cue System Preferences, and can share (or unshare) projects by using Workspace Administration. Other designers on the network must then activate Version Cue in their applications. (See "Setting up and installing Version Cue," for more information.)

If a workgroup decides to change from a user-based to a server-based implementation, projects should be migrated through backup and restore procedures to preserve complete historical versions of project files. Move the files from the user-based Version Cue Backups folder to the corresponding folder in the server-based implementation. You can move select projects or an entire user-based Workspace.

(Do not manually change the folder structure of the projects you are migrating.) You can then import the projects that have been transferred into their new Version Cue environment using Workspace Administration.

When scaling Version Cue from a single-user to a shared group environment, it is a good idea to test Version Cue before using it in real-world production. Advancing slowly gives everyone time to get used to the new technology while maintaining their productivity and preventing untimely mistakes. One strategy might be to add designers and projects only as Version Cue proves itself among current users.

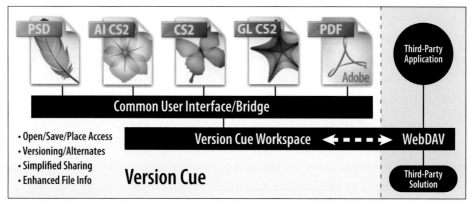

Version Cue environment: Adobe Creative Suite users can open and save file versions to the Version Cue Workspace, which connects to third-party applications via WebDAV support.

Practical limitations

Designers and system administrators may wonder what limitations to consider when using Version Cue. Unfortunately, too many variables are involved to give specific guidance. Adobe recommends that designers test Version Cue to get a qualitative understanding of how such variables as file size, number of links, and the number of users simultaneously editing files in their environment affect Version Cue. It is also sensible to take a conservative approach to rolling out Version Cue in large workgroups or workgroups that have highly complex content files.

Upgrading from a Version Cue CS (1.x) Workspace

Adobe Creative Suite CS components and Adobe CS applications will work with a Version Cue CS2 Workspace, but only to the level supported in Version Cue CS (1.x).

However, if a Version Cue CS (1.x) Workspace and a Version Cue CS2 Workspace are both installed on the same machine (which is necessary if a user has 1.x projects that must be migrated to Version Cue CS2), then Adobe CS components and Adobe CS applications will be able to find and access only a Version Cue CS (1.x) Workspace. Only upon uninstalling the Version Cue CS (1.x) Workspace will the Adobe Creative Suite components and Adobe CS applications be able to recognize and access the Version Cue CS2 Workspace installed on that machine.

Adobe Creative Suite 2 components and Adobe CS2 applications will not be able to recognize a Version Cue CS (1.x) Workspace, so users working in an environment where there are Adobe Creative Suite CS (1.x) and Adobe Creative Suite 2 users may consider waiting until there is no need for Version Cue CS (1.x) (for example, after all 1.x projects have been migrated to Version Cue CS2) before moving to a Version Cue 2 Workspace. At that point, both Adobe Creative Suite CS (1.x) components and Adobe CS applications as well as Adobe Creative Suite 2 components and Adobe CS2 applications will be able to recognize a Version Cue CS2 Workspace.

For more information

A wealth of information is available to designers, production professionals, and system administrators who want to know more about the features and capabilities of Version Cue and the technologies it uses:

- The Adobe Version Cue product page, www.versioncue.com, offers animated demos and other information about Version Cue.

- The Adobe Creative Suite product page, www.adobe.com/products/creativesuite/, shares information about all of the components of the suite and how Version Cue can be used with them.

- The Adobe Customer Support page, www.adobe.com/support/, offers searchable knowledgebase articles, user forums, training resources, and more.

- Adobe Studio®, studio.adobe.com, contains articles, case studies, tutorials, and other expert resources that help creative professionals manage the design process efficiently and maximize the value of their Adobe software.

For information on WebDAV, go to:

- www.webdav.org, a repository of WebDAV info, including articles, papers, and projects.

For more information on XMP technology, go to:

- www.adobe.com/products/xmp/, the Adobe home page for XMP information.
- http://xml.coverpages.org/xmp.html, a reference collection of information about XMP.

Index

Production Notes

The *Adobe Creative Suite 2 Classroom in a Book* was created electronically using Adobe InDesign. Art was produced using Adobe Photoshop, Adobe Illustrator, and Adobe InDesign. Proofing was completed using Adobe Acrobat 7.0 Professional using Adobe PDF files.

References to company names and telephone numbers in the lessons are for demonstration purposes only and are not intended to refer to or imply endorsement of any actual organization or person.

Typefaces used

Adobe Minion Pro and Adobe Myriad Pro are used throughout the lessons.

Team credits

The following individuals contributed to the development of the *Adobe Creative Suite 2 Classroom in a Book*:

Project coordinators, technical writers: Torsten Buck & Katrin Straub

Production: Manneken Pis Productions & Eric Geoffroy

Copyediting & Proofreading: Ross Evans

Testing: Patti D. Sokol & Manneken Pis Productions

Designer: Katrin Straub

Special thanks to Christine Yarrow, Jeffrey Warnock, Kelly Ryer & Jill Merlin.

Images

Photographic images and illustrations are provided in low-resolution formats and are intended for instructional use only. Illustrations of the Adobe InDesign user interface vary from chapter to chapter, representing Windows XP and Mac OS.

Adobe Certification

What is an ACE?

An Adobe Certified Expert (ACE) is an individual who has passed an Adobe Product Proficiency Exam for a specified Adobe software product. Adobe Certified Experts are eligible to promote themselves to clients or employers as highly skilled, expert level users of Adobe Software. ACE certification is a recognized standard for excellence in Adobe software knowledge.

ACE Benefits

When you become an ACE, you enjoy these special benefits:

- Professional recognition.

- An ACE program certificate.

- Use of the Adobe Certified Expert program logo.

What is an ACTP?

An Adobe Certified Training Provider (ACTP) is a Training professional or organization that has met the ACTP program requirements. Adobe promotes ACTPs to customers who need training on Adobe software.

ACTP Benefits

- Professional recognition.

- An ACTP program certificate.

- Use of the Adobe Certified Training Provider program logo.

- Listing in the Partner Finder on Adobe.com.

- Access to beta software releases when available.

- Classroom in a Book in Adobe Acrobat PDF.

- Marketing materials.

- Co-marketing opportunities.

previews of the images. If an external file is updated (for example, if you modify a photo in Photoshop) after it has been placed or linked to an InDesign document, InDesign will detect the change and display a warning in the Links palette. If the external file gets lost, the InDesign document will be incomplete.

One way to avoid the dependency on external files is to fully embed the file in the document (with the linked object selected, choose Embed File from the Links palette menu). However, the document file size increases with every embedded graphic, and updates to the original file are no longer automatically reflected. Considering the pros and cons, using links instead of embedding external files seems preferable. For further information, search for "embedded graphics" in the Adobe Help Center under Help for InDesign.

Exporting PDFs for online viewing

Now it is time to export the document to PDF for online viewing. All images will be downsampled to a low resolution, to reduce the file size, and colors will be converted to RGB. Since the document contains transparency (inside the native Illustrator file, placed as the masthead), the Document's Transparency Blend Space needs to be set to RGB before exporting as PDF.

1   Choose Edit > Transparency Blend Space > Document RGB.

Should you forget this step, InDesign will be kind (and smart) enough to remind you with a warning message later in the export process.

2   Choose File > Export.

3   In the Export dialog box, navigate to the Lesson04 folder, choose Adobe PDF as Format, and click Save. The Export PDF dialog box will appear.

4   In the Export PDF dialog box, select the predefined [Smallest File Size] entry from the Adobe PDF Preset pop-up menu. Choose Acrobat 7 (PDF 1.6) from the Compatibility pop-up menu. Under Options, click Optimize for Fast Web View and View PDF after Exporting. Click Export. *(See illustration on next page.)*

Note: In general, when exporting to PDF it is advisable to choose the most recent Acrobat/PDF compatibility level unless there is a specific need for backward compatibility. Most PDF files created with Acrobat 7 (PDF 1.6) compatibility can still be opened with